THOMAS WATSON ON PRAYER

31 BIBLICAL INSIGHTS FOR PIERCING HEAVEN WITH PRAYER

GODLIPRESS TEAM

CONTENTS

Introduction	vii
1. SPIRITUAL PRAYER	1
Daily Reflection	3
2. HARDSHIPS MAKE US PRAY	5
Daily Reflection	7
3. PRAYING IN FAITH	9
What Is Praying in Faith?	9
When Is It a Prayer of Faith?	10
How Do We Pray in Faith?	12
Daily Reflection	12
4. BEING VIOLENT IN PRAYER	14
Timid in Prayer	15
Daily Reflection	16
5. PRAYING FOR SPIRITUAL THINGS	18
Daily Reflection	21
6. THE THRONE AND THE HIGH PRIEST	22
Coming to the Throne	22
A High Priest Interceding	24
Daily Reflection	25
7. PRAYING FOR THE KINGDOM	26
Daily Reflection	29
8. IN THE MORNING	31
Daily Reflection	34
9. THE SPIRIT IN US	35
Daily Reflection	39
10. HONOR BEFORE REQUEST	40
Daily Reflection	42

11. ENCOURAGEMENT TO PRAY IN FAITH	44
Daily Reflection	47
12. EFFECTIVE PRAYER	49
Faith Is Necessary	49
Effort Is Necessary	50
Weak, But in Faith	51
Daily Reflection	52
13. WHY WE MUST BE VIOLENT IN PRAYER	53
Daily Reflection	55
14. MEDITATION AND PRAYER	57
Daily Reflection	59
15. PRAYER BRINGS CONTENTMENT	61
Daily Reflection	64
16. PRAYING FOR OUR NEEDS	66
Daily Reflection	68
17. WATCH AND PRAY	70
Daily Reflection	73
18. PASSIONATE AND PERSISTENT PRAYER	74
Daily Reflection	76
19. PERSEVERE IN PRAYER	78
Daily Reflection	80
20. A PRAYER OF SUBMISSION	82
Daily Reflection	84
21. CONTENT WITH ASKING FOR DAILY BREAD	86
Daily Reflection	89
22. PRAYING FOR MORE THAN BREAD	91
Daily Reflection	93
23. PRAYER OF REPENTANCE	95
Contrition	95
Confession	96
Conversion	97
Daily Reflection	98

24. FORGIVE US OUR SINS	100
Daily Reflection	102
25. IN THE FACE OF TEMPTATION	104
Overcoming Temptation	105
Daily Reflection	107
26. DELIVERANCE FROM EVIL	109
Only God Can Deliver	111
Daily Reflection	112
27. PRAYING TO BE DELIVERED	113
Daily Reflection	116
28. HUMILITY IN PRAYER	118
Daily Reflection	120
29. PRAYING FOR OTHERS	122
Daily Reflection	124
30. PRAYING FOR PASTORS	126
Daily Reflection	128
31. PRAY FOR UNITY	130
Daily Reflection	133
About Thomas Watson	135
Bibliography	137

© **Copyright 2024 by GodliPress. All rights reserved.**

This book is copyright-protected. It is only for personal use. You cannot amend, distribute, sell, use, quote, or paraphrase any part or the content within this book, without the consent of the author or publisher, except in the case of brief quotations embodied in critical articles or reviews.

Scripture quotations are from The ESV® Bible (The Holy Bible, English Standard Version®), copyright © 2001 by Crossway, a Good News Publishers publishing ministry. Used by permission. All rights reserved.

INTRODUCTION

There are always people who inspire us and stand tall as beacons to light our way toward better understanding and a closer relationship with Jesus. We hang onto every sentence they have written and every word they spoke, just to grasp a little of the insight they had into the Bible and God.

But who inspired these great people? Who did classic preachers and writers like Charles Spurgeon look up to? Who did pastors in the 1800s see as their inspiration?

Men like Thomas Watson! Having stood up to the political pressure of his day, when he was banned from preaching and continued on regardless, his tenacity and passion for the Gospel have made him one of the key figures of sound doctrine and Christianity of his age. It's one of the reasons his works have stood the test of time, hundreds of years later, and are still being published, read, and used by anyone seeking a clear and vivid picture of Christianity. And

Watson's writings do not disappoint. His colorful explanations and perceptive thoughts make him as relevant today as he was back in England centuries ago.

His writing is not only filled with biblical insights but also with classical quotes, vivid descriptions, and anecdotes that make every aspect clear and understandable. Watson had a talent for stringing together many ideas into one seamless thought. His education and his brilliant mind, infused with guidance from the Holy Spirit, made him one of the most prominent Christian authors of his time.

As a modern generation, we are spoiled to not only be able to turn to Charles Spurgeon and Andrew Murray but also to the older classics like Watson. It is why this book is such a treasure. Combining some of the extracts from his books and portions of sermons, you will find hidden nuggets and surprising analogies that will challenge and inspire you just as they have for so many other people over the years.

Who better to learn prayer from than someone who was so committed to it that it was where he was found when he died —in his time of private prayer! Watson had gone off to be alone with God, and when he did not return for a long time, he was discovered dead, still in the act of prayer. When Bishop Richardson once heard him pray, he was so moved, he followed him home to thank him and ask for a copy of his prayer. But Watson only replied, "That is what I cannot give; for I do not pen my prayers; it was no studied thing but uttered as God enabled me from the abundance of my heart and affections."

Watson may have been clever, showing amazing intellect in his writing and preaching, but it would never have had the same power and reality if it did not all come from a life of prayer. As he said himself, "A godly man will as soon live without food, as without prayer." This book delves into the mind and heart of someone who lived and breathed prayer.

The 31-day devotion format of this book makes it even easier to be able to grasp some of the truths Watson left behind for us. Using modern English for modern readers like yourself, every care has been taken to retain the same thoughts and insights without losing anything in translation. It is only to make his words accessible to current generations so we can benefit as well. Along with this, daily reflections have been added as a bonus for you to dive even deeper into understanding Watson's ideas and what they might mean in your own personal prayer life.

The sole purpose of this book, as was Watson's all those hundreds of years ago, is to challenge and encourage you into more effective and powerful prayer that can pierce heaven.

> "That prayer is most likely to pierce heaven, which first pierces one's own heart."

1

SPIRITUAL PRAYER

Praying at all times in the Spirit, with all prayer and supplication
–Ephesians 6:18

A godly person is a praying person. *"Let everyone who is godly offer prayer to you"* (Psalm 32:6). As soon as grace is poured in, prayer is poured out. Prayer is the soul's traffic to heaven—God comes down to us by His Spirit, and we go up to Him by prayer.

A spiritual prayer is a believing prayer: *"Whatever you ask in prayer, you will receive, if you have faith"* (Matt. 21:22). The reason why so many prayers are shipwrecked is that they crash against the rock of unbelief—praying without faith is shooting without bullets.

A spiritual prayer is a holy prayer: *"Men should pray, lifting holy hands"* (1 Tim. 2:8). Prayer must be offered on the altar of a pure heart. Sin makes the heart hard, and God's ear deaf. Sin stops the mouth of prayer like a kidnapper puts a gag in his captive's mouth so that he cannot speak: *"If I had cherished iniquity in my heart, the Lord would not have listened"* (Psalm 66:18). It is foolish to pray against sin, and then to sin against prayer.

A spiritual prayer is a humble prayer: *"LORD, You have heard the desire of the humble"* (Psalm 10:17 NKJV). Prayer is like begging, which requires humility. It is good to see a poor nothing lie at the feet of its Maker: *"I have undertaken to speak to the Lord, I who am but dust and ashes"* (Gen. 18:27). The lower the heart descends, the higher the prayer ascends. God accepts broken expressions when they come from broken hearts.

A spiritual prayer is when we have spiritual purposes in prayer. There is a vast difference between a spiritual prayer and a fleshly desire: The goal of a hypocrite is carnal; he looks sideways in prayer. It is not his spiritual needs that move him, but rather lust: *"You ask and do not receive, because you ask wrongly, to spend it on your passions"* (James 4:3). The sinner prays more for food than grace—this God does not see as praying but howling. *"They do not cry to me from the heart, but they wail upon their beds; for grain and wine"* (Hos. 7:14). Prayers that have a good aim find a good answer. A godly person drives the trade of prayer that they may increase the stock of grace.

Prayer delights God's ear, it melts His heart, it opens His hand—God cannot deny a praying soul.

How hard it is to get our hearts to seek God! Jesus was in an agony at prayer (Luke 22:44). Many of us are more tired and lazy when we pray than in agony. When we are doing worldly things, we are all fire; when we are in prayer, we are all ice.

The joint prayers of Christians work for the good of the godly. *"Earnest prayer for him was made to God by the church.... And behold, an angel of the Lord stood next to him... and the chains fell off his hands"* (Acts 12:5-7). The angel brought Peter out of prison, but it was prayer that brought the angel.

The person who stops praying, stops fearing God. *"But you are doing away with the fear of God and hindering meditation before God"* (Job 15:4). A person who has given up prayer is good for any evil. When Saul had stopped asking after God, he went to the witch of Endor.

Faith is the breath of prayer—prayer is dead unless faith breathes in it. *"But let him ask in faith"* (James 1:6). *"And whatever you ask in prayer, you will receive, if you have faith"* (Matt. 21:22). Without faith it is speaking, not praying. Faith must take prayer by the hand, or there is no getting close to God. A faithless prayer is fruitless. *"They were unable to enter because of unbelief."* This is the same for prayer —it cannot enter into heaven because of unbelief (Heb. 3:19).

Daily Reflection

These daily reflections are for your benefit, to allow you to think more, ask more, and learn more about prayer in your own life. You can stay on one question or work through them all, it's up to you. They are merely signposts to help you reflect on your personal response to what you have read.

Prayer is not simply talking. It is not just putting our wishes and thoughts into words. There is much more. It is spiritual. This means it involves more than our minds; it has a lot to do with our souls, our hearts, and our spirits. If we want to talk to God, who is spirit, then we will have to do so with our own spirit. Watson lays out a few aspects of prayer for us to better understand what this communication is that we have with God.

1. How would you rate your own personal prayer life right now? Fire, ice, or somewhere in between?
2. Which one describes your prayer the most out of Watson's list: believing, holy, or humble?
3. What do you understand by the term "spiritual prayer"?
4. Why do you think prayer has such a huge impact on God, enough to delight His ear and melt His heart?
5. Why is prayer so important to the life of a Christian?

2

HARDSHIPS MAKE US PRAY

Count it all joy, my brothers, when you meet trials of various kinds, for you know that the testing of your faith produces steadfastness.
–James 1:2-3

Hardships teach us humility. We are naturally prosperous and proud, but corrections are God's corrosives to eat away the proud flesh. Jesus is the lily of the valleys (Songs 2:1). He lives in a humble heart! God brings us into the valley of tears so He can bring us into the valley of humility: *"Remember my affliction and my wanderings, the wormwood and the gall! My soul continually remembers it and is bowed down within me"* (Lam. 3:19-20). When people become proud, God has no better way than to brew a cup of wormwood for them.

Hardships are compared to thorns (Hos. 2:6), God's thorns are to prick the bubble of pride. Hardships teach us repentance: *"You have disciplined me, and I was disciplined... after I had turned away, I relented"* (Jer. 31:18-19). Repentance is the precious fruit that grows on the cross.

Hardships teach us to pray better: *"They poured out a whispered prayer when your discipline was upon them"* (Isa. 26:16). They said prayers before, now they pour out prayers. Jonah was asleep on the ship, but awake and at prayer in the whale's belly. When God lights the fire of hardship, our hearts boil over even more. God loves to have His children filled with a spirit of prayer. David, the sweet singer of Israel, never tuned his harp more melodiously, he never prayed better, than when he was in affliction. So, hardships instruct us, and will we be discontent about what is for our good?

Trials and hardships motivate the spirit of prayer. The righteous are afflicted that in their affliction they may pray. Maybe we prayed in a cold and formal way when we had health and prosperity—there were no coals on the incense. We hardly cared about our own prayers, why should God care about them? God sends a hardship or something to stir us up to take hold of Him. When Jacob was afraid of being killed by his brother, he wrestled with God, wept in prayer, and would not leave Him until He blessed him (Hos. 12:4). Many Christians have fallen asleep and need a good shaking to be woken up. The Lord uses affliction to shake us from sleeping, and wake up a spirit of prayer. *"They poured out a whispered prayer when your discipline was upon them"* (Isa. 26:16). Now their prayer pierced the heavens. In times of trouble we pray with emotion, and we never pray so passionately as when we feel our prayers. Isn't this beneficial for us?

Job kept his eyes on God in his hardship. *"The Lord has taken away"* (Job 1:21). He did not complain about his enemies or the influences of the planets. He looked beyond all second causes and saw God in the affliction, and that made him happily submit. He said, *"Blessed be the name of the LORD"* (Job 1:21). Jesus looked past Judas and Pilate to God's counsel in allowing him to be crucified, which made him say, *"Not as I will, but as you will"* (Matt. 26:39). It is useless to argue with instruments. Evil people are just tools in God's hand! *"Assyria, the rod of my anger"* (Isa. 10:5). Whoever brings hardship—God sends it! This should make us say, "May your will be done"; for whatever God does, He sees a reason for.

Daily Reflection

We all go through hardships, it's part of life. Sometimes as Christians, we have this false picture that nothing bad will ever happen to us because we are protected by God. But this is not true. Jesus said we would have hardships in this world, and sometimes, he even allows them to come into our lives, for His reasons. By fighting every trial and test that comes our way, we might end up fighting against God. Instead, we should see hardships as a reason to be on our knees, praying.

1. Why do you think God allows hardships and trials in our lives? Read James 1:2-4.
2. Why do hardships motivate us to pray? What is the benefit of this?
3. Do you embrace hardships like Job did, or do you rebuke and fight everything that comes against you?

4. Why does God use trials to correct us?
5. How is your prayer different when you are going through tough times and when you are comfortable and happy?

3

PRAYING IN FAITH

And without faith it is impossible to please him, for whoever would draw near to God must believe that he exists and that he rewards those who seek him.
–Hebrews 11:6

Praying in faith means having faith—the action suggests it is a habit. To walk a certain way means it is a principle of life, so to pray in faith suggests a habit of grace. No one can pray in faith except believers.

What Is Praying in Faith?

It is to pray for that which God has promised. Where there is no promise, we cannot pray in faith.

It is to pray in Jesus' name. *"Whatever you ask in my name, this I will do"* (John 14:13). To pray in Jesus' name is to pray with confidence in Jesus' merit. When we present Jesus to God in prayer—when we carry the slain Lamb in our arms; when we say, "Lord, we are sinners, but here is our guarantee; for Jesus' sake be favorable to us"—we come to God in Christ's name. This is praying in faith.

It is to focus our faith in prayer on God's faithfulness, believing that He hears and will help. This is taking hold of God (Isaiah 64:7). By prayer we draw near to God, by faith we take hold of him. *"They cried to the Lord"* (2 Chron. 13:14), and this was the crying of faith. They *"prevailed, because they relied on the Lord, the God of their fathers"* (v 18). Making supplication to God, and focusing the soul on God, is praying in faith. To pray and not rely on God to grant our petitions is abusing and insulting God. By praying we honor God; by not believing we insult him. In prayer we say, "Almighty, merciful Father"; by not believing, we cancel all His titles.

When Is It a Prayer of Faith?

When faith in prayer is humble. An arrogant person hopes to be heard for some worth in themselves—they are so qualified and have done good service for God, therefore they are confident God will hear them. See an example in Luke 18:11-12: *"The Pharisee, standing by himself, prayed thus: 'God, I thank you that I am not like other men, extortioners, unjust, adulterers, or even like this tax collector. I fast twice a week; I give tithes of all that I get."* This was an arrogant prayer, but a sincere heart shows humility in prayer as well as faith. *"The tax collector, standing far off, would not even lift up his eyes to heaven, but beat his breast, saying, 'God, be merciful to me, a sinner!'"* (v. 13). "God, be merci-

ful," there was faith; "*to me, a sinner,*" there was humility and a sense of unworthiness.

We may know we pray in faith when we do not have what we pray for, but we believe God will give it, and we are willing to wait for it. A Christian who has a command to pray, and a promise, is resolved to follow God with prayer and not give up. Just as Peter knocked, and when the door was not opened, continued knocking until at last it was opened (Acts 12:16). So, when a Christian prays and prays, and has no answer, he continues to knock at heaven's door, knowing an answer will come. "*You answer me*" (Psalm 86:7). Here is the person that prays in faith. Jesus says, "*Pray and not lose heart*" (Luke 18:1). A believer lets down the net of prayer when Jesus tells him, and even though he catches nothing, he will throw out the net again, believing that the blessing will come. Patience in prayer is nothing but faith lasting.

Knowing how to pray in faith, we can rebuke those who pray in formality and not in faith. We can refute those who question whether God hears or gives. "*You ask and do not receive, because you ask wrongly*" (James 4:3). James does not say, you ask for something wrong, but you ask incorrectly, and therefore you do not receive it. Unbelief clips the wings of prayer so that it will not fly to the throne of grace! The rubbish of unbelief stops the current of prayer!

When we know how to pray in faith, we can encourage others. Let us put faith to work in prayer. The farmer sows in hope—prayer is the seed we sow, and when the hand of faith scatters this seed, it brings in a fruitful crop of blessings.

Prayer is the ship we send out to heaven—when faith goes on an adventure in this ship, it brings home many blessings.

How Do We Pray in Faith?

Ask the Spirit of God. We cannot say, "Our Father," except by the Holy Spirit. God's Spirit helps us, not only to pray with sighs and groans but with faith. The Spirit carries us to God —not only to a Creator but to a Father. *"God has sent the Spirit of his Son into our hearts, crying, 'Abba! Father!'"* (Gal 4:6). *"Crying"*—the Spirit causes us to pray with passion. *"Abba! Father!"*—the Spirit helps us to pray with faith. The Spirit helps faith to turn the key of prayer, and then it unlocks heaven.

Daily Reflection

The whole Christian life is built around faith, so it is understandable that we would need faith when we pray to God, read the Bible, and worship. Faith is an important part of prayer. Without it, we speak empty words we don't believe. Even worse, we don't believe anyone listens to us or will answer us. There are many people who speak simply because they have been taught to do so or it is expected of them to do it. But these are words to appease God or to make us feel better about ourselves. Praying in faith means engaging our minds and hearts, knowing that God is listening.

1. What is your definition of faith? Read Hebrews 11:1 to see the Bible's definition.

2. How much faith do you have when you pray? Is it strong, or weak and unsure?
3. Why do you think focusing on God's faithfulness is so important when praying in faith?
4. Why does Watson insist that a prayer of faith must be humble?
5. Why does Watson say we need to ask the Spirit in order to pray in faith?

4

BEING VIOLENT IN PRAYER

From the days of John the Baptist until now the kingdom of heaven has suffered violence, and the violent take it by force.
–Matthew 11:12

We need to be violent in our prayers.

Prayer is a duty that keeps devotion flowing. Whether we join with others in prayer or pray alone, we must use holy violence. It is not eloquence in prayer but violence that carries it. Theodorus said, "Once, I overheard Luther in prayer: with what life and spirit he prayed! It was with so much reverence, as if he were speaking to God—yet with so much confidence as if he had been speaking to his friend." Our hearts must be stirred **to** prayer and **in** prayer.

Our hearts must be stirred and motivated **to prayer**. *"If you prepare your heart, you will stretch out your hands toward him"* (Job 11:13). This is the preparation of our heart by holy thoughts and ejaculations. The musician first tunes his instrument before he plays.

Our hearts must be stirred and motivated **in prayer.** Prayer is lifting up the mind and soul to God, which cannot be done correctly without being violent with ourselves. The names given to prayer imply violence. It is called wrestling (Gen. 32:24), and a pouring out of the soul (1 Sam. 1:15). These imply vehemency. Emotion is required as well as intention. James speaks of an effective and powerful prayer (James 5:16), which is a similar phrase to a violent prayer.

Timid in Prayer

It is sad to see how far some people are from being violent with themselves in prayer—they give God a dead, heartless prayer. God would not have the blind offered (Mal. 1:8); as good an offer the blind is as offering the dead. Some are half asleep when they pray, and will a sleepy prayer ever wake God up? These people do not care about their own prayers, how do they think that God should care about them? Those prayers God likes best come boiling hot from the heart.

It is sad to see how far some people are from being violent in prayer—they give God distracted prayer. While they are praying, they are thinking of their work and business. How can the person whose eye is off the target shoot right? *"Their heart is set on their gain"* (Ezek. 33:31). Many are giving their lists in prayer, as Hieram once complained about himself. How can God be pleased with this? Will a king tolerate that, while his subject is delivering a petition, and speaking to him, he should be playing with a feather? When we send our hearts on an errand to Heaven, how often do they stop and play on the way? This is a matter of embarrassment.

Prayer without passion and violence is not prayer—it is speaking, not praying. Lifeless prayer is not prayer just like a picture of a person is not a real person. To say a prayer is not to pray—Ashanius taught his parrot the Lord's Prayer. It is the violence and wrestling of the emotions that make it a prayer; otherwise, it is not prayer.

If you want to be violent for heaven—continue with daily prayer. Prayer is the fan that kindles and stirs up emotions. A Christian is most active when his devotion is violent. Prayer keeps our devotion going. Prayer is to the soul, as the heart is to the body; the heart makes the body agile and alive; so does prayer for the soul. For the movement of a wristwatch to be quicker, the spring must be wound up. Christian, wind up your heart every day with prayer. Prayer brings strength from Jesus. When His strength comes in, it sets the soul to work. Prayer puts the heart in a holy attitude as the morning sun brings warmth to the room for the rest of the day. When Christians don't pray and forget about it or are not passionate about it, then they begin to lose their holy violence bit by bit.

Daily Reflection

Being violent in prayer has nothing to do with physical harshness or being angry. Some people like to wave their hands or jump about when they pray. Some get really loud, even shouting at the devil as if that would scare him away. But none of these are being violent in prayer. Watson understands it as an aggressive and intense approach to seeking after God, one in which we never let go, like a beggar or a dog, intent on getting what it came for. We need to have the same attitude in our prayers.

1. What is the difference between being motivated **to** prayer and being motivated **in** prayer?
2. Which category do your prayers fall into? Are they more timid and quiet, or are they filled with passion and wrestling?
3. Do you often struggle with being distracted in prayer? Why does this happen?
4. Why do you think praying every day is the one way to encourage violence for heaven?
5. Watson is very clear that if there is no violence in prayer, it is not really prayer. Do you agree?

5

PRAYING FOR SPIRITUAL THINGS

I will pray with my spirit, but I will pray with my mind also.
−1 Corinthians 14:15

There is a huge difference between praying for physical things and spiritual things. In praying for spiritual things, we must be clear and certain. When we pray for forgiveness of sin, the favor of God, and the gifts of the Spirit, which are necessary for salvation, we must not accept denial. But, when we pray for physical things, our prayers must be limited. We must pray conditionally—so far as God sees those things are good for us. He sometimes has a reason to hold back physical things from us—when they are traps and draw our hearts from Him. So, we should pray for these things with submission to God's will. It was Israel's sin that they were impulsive and committed to their desire for physical things. God's provisions did not please them, they wanted delicacies. *"Who will give us meat to eat?"* (Num. 11:18). God gave them manna, and He fed them with a miracle from heaven, but their greedy appetites craved more—they wanted quail. God gave them what they wanted, but they did not enjoy their quail. *"While the food was still in their mouths, the anger of God rose against them, and he killed the strongest of them"* (Psalm 78:30-31). Rachel was persistent in her desire for a child. *"Give me children, or I shall die!"* (Gen. 30:1). God let her have a child, but it became a son of my sorrow—it cost her her life. We must pray for physical things with submission to God's will; otherwise, they come in anger.

When we pray for things in our lives, we must desire physical things for spiritual goals. We must desire these things to help us in our journey to heaven. If we pray for health, it must be for God's glory, so we can be healthier for his service. If we pray for wealth, it must be for a holy reason, so we are kept from the temptations poverty exposes us to, and that we can sow seeds of charity, and help those in need. Physical things must be prayed for spiritual ends. Hannah prayed for a child, but it was for this reason: that her child might be devoted to God. *"O LORD of hosts, if you will indeed look on the affliction of your servant and remember me and not forget your servant, but will give to your servant a son, then I will give him to the LORD all the days of his life"* (1 Sam. 1:11). Many pray for physical things only to gratify their sensual appetites. To pray for these things only to satisfy us, is to cry more like ravens than Christians (Psalm 147:9). We must have a higher end in our prayers, we must aim at heaven while we are praying for the earth.

How selfish and wicked are those who beg for physical mercies that they can sin against God even more? *"You ask wrongly, to spend it on your passions"* (James 4:3). A person is sick; he prays for health so he can go and drink and be with prostitutes! Another person prays for wealth to not only fill his stomach, but also his barns. He wants to be rich to have a good name, or to have the power to take revenge on his enemies. It is immorality mixed with arrogance, to pray for God to give us physical things to be able to serve the devil better.

If we pray for physical things, how much more should we pray for spiritual things? If we pray for bread, how much more for the bread of life? If we pray for oil, how much more for the oil of gladness? If we pray to have our hunger satisfied, how much more should we pray to have our souls saved? What if God should hear our prayers and give us these physical things and nothing else—how would we be better? What good is it to have food, but not grace? What good is it to have clothes on our bodies, but leave our souls naked? To have a rich land, but not have the living springs in Jesus' blood?

So, let us be sincere when we ask for spiritual blessings! Lord, do not only feed me but sanctify me! Rather give me a heart full of grace than a house full of gold. If we are to pray for daily bread and the things of this life, we should pray even more for the things of the life that is to come.

Daily Reflection

Most of us come to God with long lists of things we need and even longer ones of the things we want! Most times, though, these lists are all about our physical necessities: paying off debts, finding work, healing for someone, food on the table. None of these are wrong, as they are all good things. But, they are limited to daily provisions that will only satisfy us physically. Watson insists we need to start praying for spiritual needs more. He sees this as far more important. The only reason we should ask for our physical needs to be met is if they will help in reaching a spiritual goal!

1. If you broke your prayer up into percentages, how much of it would be asking for physical needs to be met? How much on spiritual things?
2. Why do you think we must not accept "No" as an answer to spiritual concerns, but be content with a denial of other things?
3. What was the outcome of God giving people their desires (like Rachel and the Israelites in the desert)?
4. Why do you think humans are more focused on meeting their immediate, temporary needs than spiritual ones?
5. Why is it alright to ask for health and wealth if it meets a spiritual need?

6

THE THRONE AND THE HIGH PRIEST

Let us then with confidence draw near to the throne of grace, that we may receive mercy and find grace to help in time of need.
–Hebrews 4:16

The door of Heaven is always open for the prayers of God's people.

Coming to the Throne

If God is our Father, we can happily go to the throne of grace. If we were to ask something from our enemy, we would not have hope of getting it. But, when a child asks his father, he can hope with confidence to succeed. The word "Father" works on God—it touches His heart. How can a father deny his child? *"If his son asks him for bread, will give him a stone?"* (Matt. 7:9). This will give us the confidence to go to God for the forgiveness of sin, for more grace. We pray to a Father of mercy sitting on a throne of grace! *"If you then, who are evil, know how to give good gifts to your children, how much more will the heavenly Father give the Holy Spirit to those who ask him!"* (Luke 11:13). This motivates the church, and gives wings to prayer. *"Look down from heaven... For you are our Father"* (Isaiah 63:15-16). Who does God keep His mercies for? His children.

Three things give us confidence in prayer:

1. We have a Father to pray to.
2. We have the Spirit to help us to pray.
3. We have an Advocate to present our prayers.

God's children should run to their heavenly Father in all their troubles, just as the sick child in 2 Kings 4:19: *"He said to his father, 'Oh, my head, my head!'"* So, pour out your complaints to God in prayer. "Father, my heart, my heart! My dead heart—revive it again! My hard heart—soften it in Jesus' blood! Father, my heart, my heart!" Surely God, who hears the cry of birds, will hear the cry of His children!

This will motivate us in our prayers. Our lazy hearts need to be more spiritual. Blunt tools need sharpening, and a slow animal needs spurs to get it going. Our hearts are dull and heavy in the things of God, therefore we need to spur them on, and motivate them to that which is good. The flesh stops us from praying. When we should pray, the flesh resists; when we should suffer, the flesh draws back. How hard it is to get our hearts to seek God!

Jesus Christ went more willingly to the cross than we do to the throne of grace.

So, shouldn't we motivate ourselves more to pray? If our hearts are so unstrung, we need to put them in tune.

A High Priest Interceding

We have a friend in the throne room who puts in a good word for us and is following our case in heaven. This should encourage us in prayer. If we come in our own names in prayers, it would be presumptuous, but Jesus intercedes for us in the power of His blood. To be afraid to come to God in prayer is dishonoring His intercession. Jesus is at work for you in heaven. He intercedes for you. He *"makes intercession for the transgressors"* (Isa. 53:12). Did Jesus open up His body for you, and will He not open His mouth to plead for you?

Don't be discouraged if you have offended the High Priest by not trusting His blood, abusing His love, or grieving His Spirit, you still have a part in Jesus' prayer. *"The people of Israel grumbled against Moses and against Aaron,"* but even though they had sinned against their high priest, Aaron ran in and *"stood between the dead and the living"* (Num. 16:41, 48). If Aaron did this for the people, how much more will Jesus pray for those who have sinned against their High Priest! Didn't He pray for them that crucified him, *"Father, forgive them"* (Luke 23:34)?

The work of Jesus' intercession is a work of free grace. His praying for us is from His sympathy for us. He doesn't look at our worth, but at our needs.

Even if you are tempted, Jesus prays, and Satan will be defeated. You might lose one battle, but not the victory. Jesus prays that your faith will not fail, therefore Christian, say, *"Why are you cast down, O my soul"* (Psalm 43:5). Jesus intercedes. We sin, and God prays. The Greek word for advocate means a comforter. It is an incredible comfort that Jesus intercedes for us.

Daily Reflection

If you have a notebook, use it during these times of reading through the passages and as you work through the daily reflections. It is good to make notes of verses that stand out to you, thoughts you might have on a topic, questions you want to ask, or even objections you might have. Too often, we read, think things in our heads, and then forget them soon after. If you write them down, you can come back to them, pursue the answers you are looking for, look up the verses again, or see exactly what you were thinking. Journals have been known to increase learning and understanding, so try using a notebook.

1. What is the throne of grace, and who sits on it? You may need to do some research on this if you are not familiar with it. Reading Hebrews 4 is a good start.
2. Why can we be confident when we pray and come to the throne of grace?
3. What are the reasons we sometimes are not confident in our prayers to God?
4. Who is the High Priest, and why is this a significant role for us in our prayers? Again, read Hebrews 4.
5. How does understanding the role of the High Priest help us in our prayers?

7

PRAYING FOR THE KINGDOM

Your kingdom come.
–Matthew 6:10

We should eagerly pray, *"Your kingdom come."*

- Because it is a kingdom worth praying for. It exceeds the glory of all earthly kingdoms. Heaven is a kingdom worth praying for, nothing is lacking in that kingdom that will complete our happiness. Where do we find happiness? Is it knowledge? You *"shall know fully, even as I have been fully known"* (1 Cor. 13:12). Is it in royal food? We will be at the *"marriage supper of the Lamb"* (Rev. 19:9). Is it in rich clothing? We shall be *"clothed in white robes"* (Rev. 7:13). Is it in exquisite music? We will hear the choir of angels singing. Is it in dominion? We will reign as kings, and judge angels. Is it pleasure? We will enter into the joy of our Lord. Surely this kingdom is worth praying for! "Your kingdom come." If God gave us a vision of heaven, as He did to Stephen, who saw *"the heavens opened"* (Acts 7:56), we would be overwhelmed! *"You make known to me the path of life; in your presence there is fullness of joy; at your right hand are pleasures forevermore"* (Psalm 16:11).

- We must pray for this kingdom of glory because God will not give it to us without prayer. *"To those who... seek for glory and honor and immortality"* (Romans 2:7); and how do we seek but by prayer? God has promised a kingdom, and in prayer, we must hold Him to it. God is not so foolish as to throw away a kingdom on those who do not ask for it!
- We must pray that the kingdom of glory may come, that by going into it we will be finished with sinning. How amazing it will be to never again have a sinful thought! We must pray, *"Your kingdom come,"* for holy reasons that the shackles of evil can be taken off, and we can be like the angels who never sin. This is what made the church pray in Revelation 22:20, *"Come, Lord Jesus!"*
- Because all Christ's enemies will be put under His feet. The devil will have no more power to tempt, nor wicked men to persecute; the anti-Christian hierarchy will be pulled down, and Zion's glory will shine like a lamp.
- We must pray for the kingdom of glory to come, so we can see God face to face, and have uninterrupted and eternal communion with him in heaven. Moses wanted to have a glimpse of God's glory (Exod.

33:18). We should pray to see Him in all His robes of glory when He will shine ten thousand times brighter than the sun! Seeing and enjoying God will be the diamond in the ring, the very quintessence of glory! And must we pray, *"Your kingdom come"*? God gives some people daily bread even though they never pray for it, but He will not give the kingdom of heaven to those who never pray for it! God may feed them, but He will never crown them.

Only believers can genuinely pray for the kingdom of glory to come soon.

People who never had the kingdom of grace set up in their hearts cannot pray for Jesus' kingdom of glory to come. Can the guilty prisoners pray that the trial may come? Lovers of the world cannot pray for the heavenly kingdom. They have found paradise, they are in their kingdom already—this is their heaven, and they don't want another one. They cannot pray that Jesus' kingdom of glory may come, because then Jesus will judge them; and if they say this prayer, they are hypocrites, they do not mean what they say.

But if you have the kingdom of grace in your hearts, pray that the kingdom of glory will come soon. When Jesus' kingdom comes, the bodies of the Christians that are in the grave will be raised in honor and made like Jesus' glorious body. Then your souls are like diamonds and sparkle with holiness. You will never have sinful thoughts anymore, you shall be as holy as the angels. You will be as holy as you want to be, and as holy as God wants you to be. When Jesus' kingdom of glory comes, you will be rid of all your enemies, as Moses said,

"For the Egyptians whom you see today, you shall never see again" (Exod. 14:13). All Jesus' enemies shall be put *"under his feet"* (1 Cor. 15:25). Before the wicked are destroyed, the Christians will judge them. *"Do you not know that the saints will judge the world?"* (1 Cor. 6:2). It will cut the wicked to the heart that those whom they mocked will sit as judges over them, and vote with Jesus in His judicial proceedings.

These are all reasons why you should pray for the kingdom of glory to come soon: May *"Your kingdom come."*

Daily Reflection

Most people know the Lord's Prayer by heart and unfortunately, can recite it without even thinking too hard. Even if we pay attention to some parts, like asking for bread, forgiving our sins, and keeping us away from temptation, much of it means very little when it is said. Watson highlights just one phrase in this passage, and shows us the importance of why we should not skip over it but make it part of our daily prayers. When we understand the significance of the kingdom in our lives as Christians, we will begin to pray more for it to come, and to come soon!

1. What is your picture of heaven? Reading Revelation 21 might help you.
2. Do you ever pray for heaven, or do you take it for granted that it will happen someday?
3. What do you think about Watson's statement that God will not give heaven to those who do not ask for it?

4. Watson speaks of a kingdom of grace and the kingdom of glory. What is the difference?
5. We say them together in the prayer, but do you think *"kingdom come"* and *"will be done"* are in any way linked?

8

IN THE MORNING

O LORD, in the morning you hear my voice.
–Psalm 5:3

Why is it good to pray in the morning?

Because in the morning, the mind is in the best shape for spiritual duties—that is when Christians are themselves. Tired devotion happens at night when a person is exhausted from work! They will be better off sleeping than meditating. The morning is the queen of the day—the imagination is sharpest, the memory strongest, the spirits freshest, the body most refreshed, having restored its strength by sleep. It is a good rule: The best time to serve God is when we find ourselves most in tune. In the morning, the heart is like a violin—strung and put in tune, and then it makes the sweetest melody.

The morning thoughts stay the longest with us throughout the day. The wool absorbs the first color dye the best and is not easily worn out. When the mind receives good thoughts in the morning, it holds this sacred dye much better—like an ingrained color, it will not be easily lost. The heart keeps the pleasure of morning meditations like a cup receives the flavor and savor of the wine which is first put into it, or like linen in a cedar chest which keeps the scent for a long time. Perfume your mind with heavenly thoughts in the morning and it will not lose its spiritual fragrance! Wind up your heart toward heaven in the beginning of the day and it will go better for the rest of the day. It is the same as receiving thoughts into the mind as it is welcoming guests into a hotel —the first guests will get the best rooms in the house, while those that come later get the worst rooms. In the same way, when the mind entertains holy meditations for its morning guests, if earthly thoughts come in later, they are put into the worst rooms—they are given the lowest attention. The best rooms are taken in the morning for Jesus. If the first thing that happens in the day is you lose your heart in the world, you will not find it again so easily during the rest of the day.

It is a part of the respect and honor we give to God—to let him have the first thoughts of the day. We give people of quality the best treatment—we let them take the first place. If we honor God (whose name is holy) we will let the thoughts of God take first place. When the world has the first of our thoughts, it is a sign the world is our priority, we love it the most. The first thing a covetous man meditates on in the morning is his money—a sign his gold is close to his heart. Christians, let God have your morning meditations.

He is insulted when the world is served before him. Imagine a king and a criminal eating in the same room, sitting at two different tables. If the criminal had his food served first, the king would be disrespected and see it as an insult. When the world is served first with our morning thoughts focused on it, and the Lord is given the leftovers of the day when our thoughts are running low—isn't this an insult to the God of glory?

God deserves the first of our thoughts. Some of His first thoughts were about us—before we existed, He thought about us. *"Before the foundation of the world"* (Eph. 1:4). Before we fell, He was thinking about how to raise us. We were the morning of His thoughts. What thoughts of free grace, what thoughts of peace He has had toward us! We have taken up His thoughts since eternity. If we have been some of God's first thoughts, surely our first thoughts should be about him.

We should copy the pattern of the early Christians. Job rose early in the morning and offered a sacrifice (Job 1:5). David, when he awoke, was with God (Psalm 139:17)—this is the way to have a morning blessing. *"In the morning dew lay around"* (Exod. 16:13). The dew of a blessing falls early—then we are most likely to have God's company. If you want to meet with a friend, you go early in the morning before he goes out. The Holy Spirit came down on the apostles in the morning because it says that when they gathered afterward for Peter's sermon, it was *"only the third hour of the day"* (Acts 2:15). The morning is the time for fruitfulness—*"make them blossom in the morning that you sow"* (Isaiah 17:11). In morning meditation, we make the seed of grace grow and flourish.

Daily Reflection

When is the best time to pray? It's a question we often ask, trying to squeeze our spiritual duties into an already-crammed day. Each of us has different circumstances and responsibilities, and someone working night shifts might disagree with early mornings as the best time for prayer. It's not a rule, but more a tried-and-tested habit or technique that works best for most people. The examples in the Bible often have people praying early in the morning, but some are on their knees during the night as well. It depends on what works best in your situation, to focus your mind on God for the day.

1. When do you find the best time for you to pray?
2. Looking at the reasons Watson gives, what are the reasons that he proposes the morning as the best time to pray?
3. What do you make of the analogy of a king and a criminal? Do you think God is insulted when we focus on our work and other demands before Him?
4. Why is it important to have Jesus as our first thoughts of the day and not other things?
5. Read Mark 1:35 to see Jesus' pattern for going to pray. Do you struggle to get up early, while it's dark?

9

THE SPIRIT IN US

For we do not know what to pray for as we ought, but the Spirit himself intercedes for us with groanings too deep for words.
–Romans 8:26

We can know God is our Father by having His Spirit in us.

By having the **intercession** of the Spirit. He is a Spirit of prayer. *"And because you are sons, God has sent the Spirit of his Son into our hearts, crying, 'Abba! Father!'"* (Gal. 4:6). Prayer is the soul's breathing itself into the bosom of its heavenly Father. None of God's children are born dumb. The Holy Spirit fills His instrument and touches the hearts of Christians like the threads of harp strings. *"Behold, he is praying"* (Acts 9:11). But not every prayer is evidence of God's Spirit in us. Those with no grace can excel in gifts and affect the hearts of others in prayer, when their own hearts are not affected—the flute makes a sweet sound in the ears of others, but is not sensible itself.

How will we know our prayers are of the Spirit?

When they are not only vocal but mental. When they are not only gifts but groans (Rom. 8:26). The best music is in concert—the best prayer is when the heart and tongue join together in concert.

When they are passionate. *"The prayer of a righteous person has great power as it is working"* (James 5:16). When the eyes melt in prayer and the heart burns. Fervency is to prayer as fire to incense, which makes it ascend to heaven as a sweet perfume.

When prayer has faith mixed with it. Prayer is the key of heaven and faith is the hand which turns it. *"We cry, 'Abba! Father!'"* (Rom. 8:15). *"We cry,"* there is passion in prayer; *"Abba! Father!"* there is faith. The prayers that are shipwrecked are dashed on the rock of unbelief. We can know God is our Father by having His Spirit praying in us; as Christ intercedes above, so the Spirit intercedes within.

By having the **renewing** of the Spirit, which is regeneration—being born of the Spirit (John 3:5). This regenerating work of the Spirit is a transformation or change of nature. *"Be transformed by the renewal of your mind"* (Rom. 12:2). The person who is born of God has a new heart—not of substance, but qualities. The strings of a violin may be the same, but the tune is altered.

Now, there are spiritual pains and much heart-breaking for sin. It is called a circumcision of the heart (Col. 2:11). In circumcision there was a pain in the flesh, so in spiritual circumcision, there is a pain in the heart. There is much sorrow that comes from a sense of guilt and judgment. The jailor's trembling was a pain in the new birth (Acts 16:29). God's Spirit is first a spirit of bondage before a spirit of adoption. This work of regeneration spreads over the whole soul —it illuminates the mind, consecrates the heart, and reforms life! Even though regeneration is only part of it, it is in every part (1 Thess. 5:23).

Regeneration is the signature of the Holy Spirit on the soul. The born-again Christian is dressed with the jewels of the graces—the angels' glory. Regeneration is the spring of all true joy. At our first birth, we come crying into the world, but at our new birth, there is reason to rejoice. God is now our Father and we are adopted into a living hope of glory (1 Peter 1:3).

Has a regenerating work of God's Spirit happened in our souls? Are we born of another spirit, humble and holy? This is a sign of sonship, and we can say, "Our Father in heaven."

We know God is our Father by having the **conduct** of the Spirit. We are led by the Spirit. *"For all who are led by the Spirit of God are sons of God"* (Rom. 8:14). God's Spirit does not only motivate us in our regeneration but leads us on until we come to the end of our faith. It is not enough that the child has life, but he must be led every step by the parent. *"I who taught Ephraim to walk; I took them up by their arms"* (Hos. 11:3). As the Israelites had the cloud and pillar of fire to go before them, and be a guide to them, so God's Spirit is a guide to go before us, lead us into all truth, counsel us in all our doubts, and influence us in all our actions. *"You guide me with your counsel"* (Psalm 73:24). No one can call God Father but those who have the conduct of the Spirit.

Test what spirit you are led by. Those who are led by a spirit of envy, lust, and greed are not led by the Spirit of God! It would be blasphemy for them to call God their Father! They are led by the spirit of Satan, and can only say, "Our father, who is in hell."

By having the **witness** of the Spirit. *"The Spirit himself bears witness with our spirit that we are children of God"* (Rom. 8:16). This witness of the Spirit, suggesting that God is our Father, is not a vocal witness or voice from heaven. The Spirit in the Word witnesses. It says that whoever is a hater of sin and a lover of holiness is a child of God, and God is their Father. If I can find these qualifications in my heart, it is the Spirit witnessing with my spirit that I am a child of God. We can take it further. The Spirit of God witnesses to our spirit by making extraordinary impressions on our hearts and giving secret hints and whispers that God has purposes of love for us. This is a parallel witness of the Spirit with our conscience, that we are heirs of heaven, and God is our Father. This witness is better felt than expressed, it scatters doubts and fears, and silences temptations.

But what about those who do not have this witness of the Spirit? If we lack the witness of the Spirit, let us make every effort to find the work of the Spirit. If we do not have the Spirit testifying, let us make every effort to have Him sanctifying, and that will be a support to us.

Daily Reflection

The Holy Spirit is not just a force or a mystical presence, but God! The Holy Spirit is very important in prayer. Not just in prayer, but in every part of our Christian lives and our spiritual duties. It's the reason Jesus promised to send the Spirit when He returned to heaven. Jesus knew we would need help, spiritual help for spiritual things. We cannot pray or enter into our duties without the Spirit's help; otherwise, it will end up being human efforts with no spiritual use.

1. Why is the Holy Spirit so necessary for prayer?
2. Do you ever acknowledge or ask for help from the Spirit in your prayers?
3. Watson takes it further by saying that we need the Holy Spirit **in** us. What does this mean?
4. What is the evidence that the Spirit is working in us and through us?
5. What does Romans 8:26 mean?

10

HONOR BEFORE REQUEST

> Our Father in heaven, *hallowed be your name.*
> –Matthew 6:9

We must see that there is an order in prayer.

First, we pray, *"Hallowed be your name. Your kingdom come, your will be done,"* before we pray, *"Give us this day our daily bread"* (Matt. 6:9-11). God's glory should weigh down everything else before it. It must come before our own concerns. Jesus chose His Father's glory before His own as He was a man. *"I honor my Father… Yet I do not seek my own glory"* (John 8:49-50). God's glory is most precious to him; it is the apple of His eye; all His riches are there. As Micah said, *"What have I left?"* (Judges 18:24)—so we can say of God's glory, what more have we? His glory is the most valuable pearl of His crown—he will not part with it. *"My glory I give to no other"* (Isa. 42:8). God's glory is worth more than heaven, worth more than the salvation of all men's souls. It is better for kingdoms to be demolished, better for men and angels to be annihilated—than for God to lose any part of His glory!

We are to prefer God's glory before our own concerns. But before we prefer God's glory to our personal concerns, we must be born again. The natural man seeks his own interest before God's glory. He who is *"of the earth belongs to the earth and speaks in an earthly way"* (John 3:31). Let him have peace and trading, let the rock pour out rivers of oil, and let God's glory go wherever it will, he does not care. A worm cannot fly and sing like a bird. In the same way, a natural person, whose heart is set on the earth, cannot admire God or advance His glory, as a person elevated by grace does.

Do we prefer God's glory before our personal concerns?

1. We must prefer God's glory before our own reputation. Reputation is a highly valued jewel. Like precious ointment, it casts a fragrant smell. But God's glory must be better than credit or applause to us. We must be willing to have our reputation trampled so that God's glory can be lifted higher. The apostles rejoiced *"that they were counted worthy to suffer dishonor for the name"* (Acts 5:41). They were graced to be disgraced for Jesus.
2. We must prefer God's glory before our relations. Relations are dear, they are of our own flesh and bones, but God's glory must be more precious. *"If anyone comes to me and does not hate his own father and mother... he cannot be my disciple"* (Luke 14:26). Hatred

toward one's own family is devotion toward God. "If my friends," says Jerome, "should persuade me to deny Jesus, if my wife should hang about my neck, I would trample upon all and run to Jesus."

3. We must prefer God's glory before our estate. Gold is just shining dust. God's glory must weigh more. If it comes to this—I cannot hold onto my place of profit, and allow God's glory to be eclipsed—I must rather lose my estate and all I own than God's glory should suffer (Heb. 10:34).

4. We must prefer God's glory before our life. *"They loved not their lives even unto death"* (Rev. 12:11). Ignatius called his prison shackles his spiritual jewels; he wore them as a chain of pearls. Gordius the martyr said, "It is to my loss, if you reduce any of my sufferings." Grace grows and is elevated to a higher level. Only a soul full of love for God can see God on the throne and prefer him above all personal concerns.

Daily Reflection

Many of the old classic writers believed there should be an order in prayer. Today, we are often too relaxed in our approach to praying, saying whatever comes to our minds in a spontaneous way. We want to be free without rules and law, which is good since we have grace. But, there are still methods that can help us to come to God properly, with our minds and hearts in the right place, rather than rambling through whatever we feel at that moment. An order of prayer helps us to see God first, before bringing ourselves and our needs.

1. Looking at the Lord's Prayer in Matthew 6, can you see an order of prayer that Jesus was trying to teach His disciples?
2. Do you ever start your prayers by acknowledging God and who He is, or do you jump in first with your list of needs?
3. Why do you think God's glory should be given priority over our own concerns?
4. How does this change the nature of our prayers?
5. Why does Watson say this is only something a born-again person can understand and do?

11

ENCOURAGEMENT TO PRAY IN FAITH

*Therefore I tell you, whatever you ask in prayer,
believe that you have received it, and it will be yours.*
–Mark 11:24

The following points will encourage us so that we can pray in faith.

God's readiness to hear prayer. If God banned all addresses to him, it would put a stop to the business of prayer, but His ear is open to prayer. One of the names by which He is known as *"O you who hear prayer"* (Psalm 65:2). God is ready to hear and grant prayer, which should encourage faith in prayer. Some may say they have prayed but have had no answer. God can hear prayer, though He does not immediately answer it. We write a letter to a friend, he may have received it, though we have still had no answer to it. Perhaps you pray for the light of God's face; He hears you, but He does not show you His face. God might give an answer to prayer when we do not perceive it. His giving us the heart to pray, and stirring up the emotions in prayer, is an answer to prayer. *"On the day I called, you answered me; my strength of soul you increased"* (Psalm 138:3). David's inner strength was an answer to prayer. So, God's readiness to hear prayer encourages faith in prayer.

We do not pray alone. Jesus prays our prayers over again. His prayer is the foundation for why our prayer is heard. He takes the rubbish out of our prayer and presents nothing to His Father but pure gold. He mixes His sweet fragrances with the prayers of Christians (Rev. 5:8). Think of the dignity of who He is—He is God; and the sweetness of His relation —He is a Son. What an encouragement to pray in faith! Our prayers are put into the hand of a Mediator. Jesus' prayer is mighty and powerful.

We pray for what is pleasing to God, and that He wants to give it. If a son asks only what his father is willing to give, it will make him go to him with confidence. When we pray to God for holy hearts, there is nothing more pleasing to him. *"For this is the will of God, your sanctification"* (1 Thess. 4:3). We pray that God would give us hearts to love Him, and there is nothing He desires more than our love. It should make us pray in faith when we only pray for what is acceptable to God, and which He delights to give!

The many promises that God has made to prayer. A cork keeps the net from sinking, so the promises are the cork to keep faith from sinking in prayer. God has tied Himself to us by His promises. The Bible is filled with promises made to prayer.

"He will surely be gracious to you at the sound of your cry" (Isaiah 30:19)

"The same Lord is Lord of all, bestowing his riches on all who call on him" (Rom. 10:12)

"You will seek me and find me, when you seek me with all your heart" (Jer. 29:13)

"He fulfills the desire of those who fear him" (Psalm 145:19)

The Syrians tied their god Hercules with a golden chain so that he should not leave; God has tied Himself to us by His promises.

- Jesus has bought that which we pray for. We may think the things we ask for in prayer are too great for us to obtain, but they are not too great for Jesus to purchase. We pray for forgiveness. Jesus has bought it with His blood. We pray for the Spirit to renew and inspire us. The sending of the Holy Spirit into our hearts is the fruit of Jesus' death. It should put life into our prayers and make us pray in faith, to reflect that the things we ask, though they are more than we deserve, are not more than Christ has purchased for us.
- Abundance in God that He often exceeds the prayers of His people. He gives us more than we ask! Hannah asked for a son, and God not only gave her a son but a prophet. Solomon asked for wisdom, and God gave

him not only wisdom but riches and honor. Jacob prayed that God would give him food and clothes, and He increased his staff into two camps (Gen. 32:10). God is often better to us than our prayers, as when Gehazi asked for one talent of silver, Naaman had to force him to take two (2 Kings 5:23). We ask for one talent, and God gives two. The woman of Canaan asked for a crumb—the life of her child— Jesus gave her more, He sent her home with the life of her soul.

Daily Reflection

Praying in faith is not always easy. Our hearts and minds can be swayed by our emotions and thoughts much more quickly than we would like. Sometimes we just have no faith, or we are distracted and can't seem to trust that God is listening or will even answer our futile words. But, we can encourage ourselves to believe that He does hear and He will answer when we are reminded of these points that Watson lays out for us. The Bible is filled with promises and statements we can hold on to, knowing that our prayers, even if they don't feel full of faith, reach God's ears and turn His hand toward us.

1. Do you always feel full of faith and belief when you are praying? Why?
2. What builds up faith in your times of prayer?
3. Do you know any of God's promises—things He will 100% do for you? Do you ever remind yourself (and God) of these?

4. Watson says that God is an abundant God. Have you ever experienced this? Where He gives more than you asked for?
5. Read Matthew 21:22. How does this tie in with what you have been reading?

12

EFFECTIVE PRAYER

The LORD is far from the wicked, but he hears the prayer of the righteous.
–Proverbs 15:29

Faith Is Necessary

An effective prayer of faith is solid and established. Like Jonathan's bow, it has not returned empty. When we pray in faith, we overcome God. We see it in the prayer Jacob prayed: *"Deliver me"* (Gen. 32:11). These words were mixed with faith in the promise. *"You said, 'I will surely do you good'"* (v. 12). This prayer of his had power with God, and succeeded (Hos. 12:4). The prayer of faith has opened prison doors, stopped the sun, locked and unlocked heaven (James 5:17). The prayer of faith has strangled the plans of enemies, and has defeated their forces. Moses' prayer against Amalek did more than Joshua's sword. Doesn't this encourage faith in prayer?

Think how heartless it is to pray without faith—not to be effective or successful in prayer. The heart doesn't trust that God hears or gives us what we ask for. Faithless praying brings no comfort, because there is no promise given to unbelieving prayer. It is sad to sail with no place to anchor, and sad to pray with no promise to anchor upon (James 1:7). The disciples tried all night and caught nothing, so the unbeliever continues in prayer and catches nothing. They don't receive any spiritual blessings, the forgiveness of sin, or grace. As for the physical blessings which the unbeliever has, he cannot see them as the fruit of prayer, but as the overflowing of God's abundance. Therefore, make every effort to have faith in prayer!

Effort Is Necessary

How terrible it would be if you did not make it because you didn't put in enough effort! The prophet Elisha told the king of Israel to hit the ground six times, and he only struck it three times, then stopped (2 Kings 13:19). He lost many victories because of this. In the same way, when a person thinks, "I did something in religion, but did not do enough. I prayed, but it was cold-hearted—I did not put coals on the incense. I heard the word but did not meditate on it. I only struck three times, when I should have done it six times. If I had put in a little more effort, I would have been happy, but I have lost the kingdom of heaven by aiming short!" The thought of losing heaven because we did not do enough should motivate our sluggish hearts, and make us more diligent to pray to get the kingdom.

"*I give myself to prayer*" (Psalm 109:4). Prayer motivates emotions and oils the wheels of effort. Prayer succeeds with God, unlocks His affections, and then He unlocks heaven. All those who have made it to heaven have crept there on their knees. The Christians who are now in heaven have been people of prayer. Daniel prayed three times a day, and Jacob wrestled with God in prayer, and as a prince, prevailed. Prayer must be passionate; otherwise, it is, as Luther says, "A golden incense burner without fire." Follow God with prayers and tears. Say as Jacob did to the angel, "*I will not let you go unless you bless me*" (Gen. 32:26). Luther also said, "Prayer conquers the Omnipotent." Elijah by prayer opened heaven. Through wholehearted and constant prayer, heaven is opened to us.

Weak, But in Faith

Maybe your answer is, "But so much sin sticks to my prayer that I am afraid it is not the prayer of faith, and God will not hear it."

If this is your cry, know that your prayer is in faith, and God will hear it. Weakness does not make a Christian's prayers invalid. "*I had said in my alarm, 'I am cut off'*" (Psalm 31:22). There was much unbelief in that prayer. "*I had said in my alarm*" in Hebrew means "in my fear and trembling." David's faith trembled and fainted, but God heard his prayer. Christians' weaknesses do not stop their prayers (James 5:17). So, don't be discouraged, because if sin sticks to your holy offering, these two things may comfort you: You can pray with faith, even though it is with weakness; and God sees the sincerity, and will overlook the weakness.

Daily Reflection

If we said we didn't care if our prayers had any effect or not, we'd be lying. All of us hope that our prayers have some kind of consequence. If we're honest, most of us believe that our prayers are weak and selfish, and result in nothing more than the words we speak into the air. Watson believed each one of us can pray effective, powerful prayers that will not only reach heaven but bring a response. And the good news is, he understood that sometimes we are weak and have no faith, but even then, he encourages us that our prayers will be heard.

1. How would you describe an effective prayer? Do you ever pray in this way?
2. What does it mean to have a solid, established prayer?
3. Why is faith such a key aspect of a prayer being powerful and effective?
4. What does it mean to put effort into your prayers, and how is this different from simply performing duties?
5. Is it possible to pray in weakness and still be effective in the Spirit? Read Romans 8:26.

13

WHY WE MUST BE VIOLENT IN PRAYER

*The good news of the kingdom of God is preached,
and everyone forces his way into it.*
–Luke 16:16

When we are praying, we need to think about the majesty of God to whom we are addressing. He sees how it is with us in prayer, whether we are deeply affected by those things we pray for. *"The king came in to look at the guests"* (Matt. 22:11). So when we go to pray, the King of glory comes in to see what attitude we are in; He has a window which looks into our chests, and if He sees a dead heart, He might not listen. Nothing will make God's anger heat up quicker than a cold prayer.

Our passion and violence in prayer suit God's nature. He is a spirit (John 4:24), and the prayer which is full of life and spirit is the food He loves: *"Spiritual sacrifices acceptable to God"*

(1 Peter 2:5). Spirituality and fervency in duty are like the spirits of wine, which are the more refined part of the wine. Physical exercise is worth nothing. It is not the stretching of the lungs, but the forcefulness of the desire that makes music in God's ears.

It is only violence and intensity of spirit in prayer that has the promise of mercy attached to it. *"Knock, and it will be opened to you"* (Matt. 7:7). Knocking is a violent motion. The Aediles in Roman times always had their doors standing open so that everyone who had petitions could have free access to them. God's heart is always open to fervent prayer. Let us be fired with passion, and with Jesus pray even more earnestly. It is violence in prayer that makes Heaven's gates fly open and brings in whatever blessings we need.

God has given huge returns to violent prayer. The dove sent to heaven has often brought an olive leaf in its mouth: *"This poor man cried, and the Lord heard him"* (Psalm 34:6). Crying prayer succeeds. Daniel in the den prayed and succeeded. Prayer closed the lion's mouth and opened the lion's den. Fervent prayer has a kind of omnipotence in it. Sozomen said that Apollonius never asked for anything from God in all his life, which he did not get. Luther wanted to seek the Lord, so he prayed, and after a long time on his knees, he came out of his room excitedly, saying to his friends, "We have overcome; we have overcome!" At the same time, a proclamation came from Charles the Fifth, that no one should be hurt for preaching the gospel. This must encourage us to hoist up the sails of prayer when other Christians have had such good returns from the holy land.

To have holy violence in prayer, we need a renewed principle of grace. If the person is graceless, no wonder the prayer is heartless. A dead body has no heat in it—while a person is dead in sin, they can have no heat in prayer.

To be more violent in prayer, it is good to pray knowing our needs. A poor beggar will be serious about asking for money. Christian, look at your needs—you need a humble, spiritual attitude of heart; you need the light of God's face; the sense of need will motivate prayer. No one can pray fervently if they do not pray with emotion. How desperate was Samson for water when he was ready to die: *"I now die of thirst"* (Judg. 15:18).

If we are going to be violent in prayer, we must beg for a violent wind. The Spirit of God is shown as a mighty rushing wind (Acts 2:2). We are violent when this wind fills our sails. *"Praying in the Holy Spirit"* (Jude 1:20). If there is any fire in our sacrifice, let it come down from heaven.

Daily Reflection

Once again, Watson focuses on being violent in prayer. Our modern English portrays violence as something bad, like an attack or terrorism of sorts. This has caused many people to confuse the Bible verse Matthew 11:12. It does not mean taking up arms, defending ourselves physically, or lashing out against evil. Instead, it talks about an attitude we should have when praying. In the same way that soldiers would have an attitude in war, we should be in our prayers. There is no defeat, no questioning orders, but pushing on until we reach our objective—that is what it means to be violent in prayer.

1. Are you ever forceful in your prayers; not in your actions and mannerisms, but in your heart?
2. Do you think it's possible for timid, shy, introverted people to also be violent in their prayers?
3. Why do you think God honors and respects this type of violent prayer so much?
4. How do holy violence and grace go together when they seem to be opposite attributes?
5. What would you need to change in your own prayers to become more effective, violent, and forceful?

14

MEDITATION AND PRAYER

Let the words of my mouth and the meditation of my heart
be acceptable in your sight.
–Psalm 19:14

Meditation is a duty that consists of the essentials of religion and feeds the lifeblood of it. To show how much Christians should be used to meditating, the Psalmist adds, *"On his law he meditates day and night."* The godly person meditates day and night, meaning it is being done frequently —they are very familiar with the duty.

It is a command of God to pray without ceasing (1 Thess. 5:17). This does not mean that we should always be praying, but that we should set some time apart for prayer every day. We read in the Old Testament it was called the continual sacrifice (Num. 28:24). The people of Israel did not only sacrifice and nothing else but because they had their set hours, every morning and evening they offered, therefore, it was called the continual sacrifice. So, the godly person is said to meditate day and night—they do it so often that they are not strangers to it.

Meditation works with prayer. Prayer is the spiritual pulse of the soul, beating strongly after God. There is no living without prayer; a man cannot live unless he breathes. The soul cannot live unless it breathes out its desires to God.

- Prayer brings in mercy, and prayer sanctifies mercy—it makes mercy to be mercy (1 Tim. 4:5).
- Prayer has power over God (Hos. 12:4).
- Prayer comes with letters of request to heaven.
- Prayer is the spiritual leech that sucks the poison of sin out of the soul.

What a wonderful privilege prayer is! Meditation helps prayer. Gerson calls it the nurse of prayer. Meditation is like oil for the lamp—the lamp of prayer will go out unless meditation feeds it. Meditation and prayer are like two turtle doves—if you separate one, the other dies. A skillful fisherman observes the time and season when the fish bite best, and then he throws in his hook. In the same way, when the heart is encouraged by meditation, that is the best season to throw in the hook of prayer and fish for mercy. After Isaac had been in the field meditating, he was ready for prayer when he came home. When the gun is full of powder, it is ready to shoot. So, when the mind is full of good thoughts, a Christian is ready for prayers to fire, sending up shots of sighs and groans to heaven.

Meditation has a double benefit in it—it pours in, and pours out. First, it pours good thoughts into the mind, and then it pours out those thoughts again into prayer. Meditation first provides matter to pray about, and then it provides a heart to pray. *"As I mused,"* says David, and the very next words are a prayer: *"O LORD, make me know my end"* (Psalm 39:3-4). In Psalm 143:5-6, *"I meditate on all that you have done; I ponder the work of your hands. I stretch out my hands to you,"* his thinking of his head made way for the stretching out of his hands in prayer. When Jesus was on the mountain, then He prayed. In the same way, when your heart is on the mountain of meditation, it is tuned for prayer. Prayer is the child of meditation. Meditation leads the way, and prayer follows.

We must also seal meditation with prayer. Pray over your meditations. Prayer sanctifies everything. Without prayer, they are not holy meditations. Prayer tightens meditation to the heart. Prayer is a knot tied at the end of meditation so that it does not slip. Pray that God will keep those holy meditations in your mind forever, that the flavor of them may stay in your hearts. *"O LORD... keep forever such purposes and thoughts in the hearts of your people, and direct their hearts toward you"* (1 Chron. 29:18). So, let us pray that when we have been thinking about heavenly things, and our hearts are motivated within us, we may not cool into a sinful lukewarmness, but that we will be like a lamp—always burning.

Daily Reflection

Meditation was such an important aspect to Thomas Watson that he wrote a whole essay on it. This is only a small excerpt from that essay, but it still shows the importance he saw in the act of meditation. These days we have merged the ideas of prayer, reading the Bible, and meditating, so that they are all the same thing. But to Watson, they were all different parts of our worship and spiritual duties to God. They work together, but each has its specific place in bringing us closer to God and understanding His ways.

1. How are prayer and meditation different? Read Psalm 19:14 and Psalm 49:3 to help you.
2. Do you ever take time to meditate and think over what you have read in the Bible?
3. How is Christian meditation different from other forms of Eastern meditation?
4. Why do you think Watson puts meditation before prayer?
5. Why does Watson insist we should "seal" our meditations with prayer?

15

PRAYER BRINGS CONTENTMENT

But godliness with contentment is great gain, for we brought nothing into the world, and we cannot take anything out of the world.
–1 Timothy 6:6-7

Contentment is a flower that does not grow in every garden.

It would be great if there was a cure for poverty. But there is something even better—for a person to be poor, and still have enough! Contentment teaches us how to have much in the midst of poverty. Contentment is a solution for all our troubles, a relief for all our burdens, and a cure for every worry. Contentment, though not a virtue (it is an attitude), is a happy mixture of all the virtues: faith, patience, meekness, humility, etc.

Contentment makes a person in tune to serve God. It oils the wheels of the soul and makes it more agile; it composes the heart, and makes it ready for prayer, meditation, etc. How can a person who is in grief, or discontent, seek the Lord without distraction? Contentment prepares and tunes the heart. First, you prepare the violin and wind up the strings before you play music. When a Christian's heart is wound up to this heavenly attitude of contentment, then it is ready for duty.

A discontent Christian is like Saul when the evil spirit came on him—there is no harmony in prayer! When an army is thrown into chaos, it is not fit for battle; when the thoughts are scattered and distracted about the cares of this life, a person is not fit for devotion. Discontent takes the heart completely off God and focuses it on the present trouble, so that your mind is not on your prayer but on your trouble. Discontent disjoints the soul, and it is impossible for a Christian to go steadily and cheerfully in God's service. Your devotion will be deformed!

The discontent person gives God only a half-duty, and his religion is nothing but an external exercise. David never offered anything to God that cost him nothing (2 Samuel 24:24). Where there is too much worldly care, there is too little spiritual cost in a duty. The discontent person performs half-hearted duties; he is just like Ephraim, *"a cake not turned"* (Hos. 7:8), he is a cake baked only on one side. He gives God the outside but not the spiritual part—his heart is not in duty. He is baked on one side, but the other side is dough. What good is raw, undigested service? The person who gives God only the skin of worship can expect no more than the shell of comfort. Contentment brings the heart into the right attitude, and only then do we give God the flower and soul of a duty when the soul is composed.

There are some duties that we cannot perform properly without contentment:

- To rejoice in God. How can you rejoice if you are discontent? You are better off moaning than rejoicing.
- To be thankful for mercy. Can a discontent person be thankful? You can be worried, not thankful.
- To justify God in what He does. How can you do this if you are discontent with your condition? Contentment prepares the heart for duty. Contentment does not only make our duties light and easy—but acceptable to God. This is what puts beauty and worth into them, because contentment settles the soul. When milk is continually stirred, you can make nothing with it, but let it settle for a while, and then it turns to cream. When the heart is filled with discontent, you can make nothing of those duties. But when the heart is settled by holy contentment, there is some worth in our duties; now they turn to cream.
- Be in prayer. The last rule for contentment is to be in prayer. Beg God to work your hearts into this attitude. *"Is anyone among you sick?... Let them pray"* (James 5:14). In the same way, if anyone is discontent, let them pray. Prayer is an opening in the vein that lets out the bad blood. When the heart is filled with sorrow and disquiet, prayer lets out the

bad blood. The key of a prayer, oiled with tears, unlocks the heart of all its discontents! Prayer is a holy charm, to drive away trouble. Prayer is the unloading of the soul of all our cares into God's arms, and this brings sweet contentment. When there is any burden on our spirits, by opening our minds to a friend, we find our hearts are greatly comforted. It is not our strong resolutions, but our strong requests to God, which must give the heart comfort in trouble. By prayer, the strength of Jesus comes into the soul, and where that is, a man is able to go through any condition. In every different state, Paul could be content. He tells us that even though he could have nothing and have much and *"do all things,"* yet it was through Jesus strengthening him (Phil. 4:13).

Daily Reflection

Using your Bible in these reflections will help you a lot, especially since Watson refers to so many verses along the way. It is good to look them up; not just to read them and skip over them, but to find them in the actual Bible for yourself. This can help to put a single verse into context, to see the bigger picture and why those words were written or said. It also can help us to see other verses if your Bible has links to these, and this will deepen your understanding of the Scriptures.

1. Why is contentment necessary in our prayers?
2. Why does discontent cause chaos and conflict in our prayers?

3. Read 1 Timothy 6:6. Does this mean godliness is good, but being content is even better? Why?
4. Watson seems to say that prayer can bring us contentment. How is that possible?
5. Are you content when you are praying?

16

PRAYING FOR OUR NEEDS

Do not be anxious about anything, but in everything by prayer and supplication with thanksgiving let your requests be made known to God.
–Philippians 4:6

Is everything a gift? Then we should seek every blessing from God in prayer. *"Give us this day"* (Matt. 6:11). The tree of mercy will not drop its fruit unless shaken by the hand of prayer. Whatever we have, if it does not come through prayer, it does not come in the way of love; it is given, as Israel's quails, in anger. If everything is a gift, we do not deserve it. Must we go to God for every blessing? How wicked are those, who, instead of going to God for food when they want, go to the devil and make a deal with him? If he will help them, they will give him their souls! It's better to starve than go to the devil for provision.

Let us depend on God in all our trials and needs. Let us believe that He will provide for all our needs. Children rely on their parents to supply their needs. If we trust God for salvation, shouldn't we trust him for sustenance? *"Consider the ravens: they neither sow nor reap, they have neither storehouse nor barn, and yet God feeds them"* (Luke 12:24). If God feeds the birds of the air, won't He also feed His children? *"Consider the lilies, how they grow: they neither toil nor spin, yet I tell you, even Solomon in all his glory was not arrayed like one of these"* (v. 27). If God clothes the lilies, won't He also clothe His lambs? Even the wicked taste of His abundance. *"Their eyes swell out through fatness"* (Psalm 73:7). If God feeds His slaves, won't He also feed His family?

His children may not have an equal share in the things of this life. They may only have a little meal in the pot; they may have run low, and almost dry; but they will have as much as God sees is good for them. *"Those who seek the Lord lack no good thing"* (Psalm 34:10). If God does not give them what they want, He will give them what is good for them. If He does not give them what they always crave, He will give them what they need. If He does not give them a feast, He will give them enough along the way. Let them depend on His fatherly provision. Let them not have thoughts of mistrust, distracting worries, or sinful ways. *"Casting all your anxieties on him, because he cares for you"* (1 Peter 5:7).

An earthly parent might love his child, and will gladly provide for him, but might not be able to do so. God is never at a loss to provide for His children, and He has promised an adequate supply. *"Verily thou shalt be fed"* (Psalm 37:3 KJV). Will God give His children heaven, but not give them enough to get there? Will He give them a kingdom, and deny them daily bread? Put your trust in Him, for He has said, *"I will never leave you nor forsake you"* (Heb. 13:5).

Think about those things we really need that we ask for in prayer. We come to ask the favor of God; and if we do not have His love, all that we enjoy is cursed to us. We pray that our souls may be washed in Jesus' blood, and if He does not wash us, we *"have no share with"* Him (John 13:8). If God denies us these blessings, we are forever lost. So, what persistence do we need to put in our prayers when we ask? When will we be sincere, if not when we are begging for our lives?

This should motivate us to be forceful in prayer, knowing that those things which we ask, God wants to give us. If a son asks only what his father is willing to give, he can be more persistent in asking. We go to God for the forgiveness of sin, and nothing is more pleasing to Him than to forgive. Mercy is His delight (Mic. 7:18). We pray to God for a holy heart, and this prayer is according to His will. *"For this is the will of God, your sanctification"* (1 Thess. 4:3). We pray that God will give us a heart to love Him. How pleasing this request is to God! This, if anything, may encourage and motivate prayer, and carry it in a fiery chariot up to Heaven: when we know we only pray for that which God is more willing to give than we are to ask.

Daily Reflection

Most of us have no problem praying for our own needs. It's the first thing we do when we come to God. We have long lists of things we want and things we need Him to do for us. The good news is that God is willing and wants to give us what we need. We are His children and He will look after us as a father. This should bring us faith and encouragement so that we can bring all our petitions to Him, knowing that He is good and faithful to give us what we need.

1. Do you see everything as a gift from God or as something that you have a right to? What is the difference?
2. How is God different from earthly fathers? Does this change the way we come to Him?
3. Why do we need God's love more than receiving what we ask for?
4. What pleases God more, asking for physical needs or for spiritual needs?
5. Watson says we may not have everything we want, and may even lack things. How does this line up with God wanting to give us things?

17

WATCH AND PRAY

Watch and pray that you may not enter into temptation.
–Matthew 26:41

If you want to go to heaven, you must keep watch every day. *"I say to all: Watch!"* (Mark 13:37 NKJV). Many have lost heaven because they were not awake and alert. Our hearts are ready to deceive us into sin, and the devil waits to ambush us with his temptations. We must set a guard every day, and keep a lookout in our souls. *"I will take my stand at my watchpost"* (Hab. 2:1).

We must watch our eyes. *"I have made a covenant with my eyes"* (Job 31:1). A lot of sin comes in through the eye. When Eve saw that the tree was good for food, and pleasing to the eyes, she took it (Gen. 3:6). First she looked—then she lusted. The eye, by seeing an impure object, sets the heart on fire. The devil often creeps in at the window of the eye. Watch your eyes!

Watch your ears. A lot of poison comes in through the ear. Let your ears be open to God—and closed to sin.

Watch your hearts. We are alert and watchful around suspicious people. *"The heart is deceitful above all things, and desperately sick"* (Jer. 17:9). Watch your heart in the following ways:

When you are busy with holy things, it can slip into vanity. "When I am at prayer," says Jerome, "either I am walking through galleries or bringing up accounts."

Watch your hearts when you are in the company of others. The wicked are infectious, but also watch your hearts when you are in good company. The devil is subtle, and he can creep into the dove just as he did into the serpent. Satan tempted Jesus through one of His own disciples.

Watch your hearts in prosperity. Now you are in danger of pride. The higher the river rises, the higher the boat is lifted up. In the same way, the higher people's wealth rises, the higher their hearts are lifted up in pride. In prosperity, you are in danger not only of forgetting God but lifting up your heel against him. *"Jeshurun grew fat, and kicked"* (Deut. 32:15). It is hard to carry a full cup without spilling. In the same way, it is hard to carry a full, prosperous property without sinning. Just as Samson fell asleep in Delilah's lap, so many have fallen fast asleep in the lap of prosperity—they did not wake up until they were in hell!

Watch your hearts after spiritual duties. After Jesus had been praying and fasting, the devil tempted him (Matthew 4:3).

After fighting with Satan in prayer, we can feel safe and take our spiritual armor off—then the devil attacks and wounds us! If you want to get to heaven, always be on your watchtower; set a guard, keep a close lookout of your souls. Who wouldn't want to watch when it is for a kingdom?

If you would be kept from actual sins, be continually on your spiritual watch.

Watch your thoughts. *"How long shall your wicked thoughts lodge within you?"* (Jer. 4:14). Sin begins with the thoughts. First, men feed thoughts of revenge, then they dip their hands in blood. Set a guard over your thoughts.

Watch your passions of anger and lust. The heart is ready to be destroyed by its own passions, as a vessel to be overturned by its sails. Passion takes you beyond reason. Anger is temporary insanity. Moses in a passion *"spoke rashly with his lips"* (Psalm 106:33). The disciples in a passion, wanted to call down fire from heaven. A man in a passion is like a ship in a storm that has no captain or sails to help it—it is exposed to waves and rocks.

Watch your temptations. Satan always lies in ambush and watches to lure us to sin. The devil stands ready for battle. He is always fishing for our souls. He is always laying snares and shooting darts. Therefore, we must watch him and be alert, so that we are not deceived into sin. Most sin is committed because we are not alert and praying. *"Be watchful. Your adversary the devil prowls around like a roaring lion, seeking someone to devour"* (1 Peter 5:8).

Daily Reflection

It is one thing to pray and hand over everything to God, hoping He will take care of it all for us. But, we also need to be diligent and awake in our hearts. We cannot ask God to keep us from sin, but we are lazy when it comes to temptation, and then wonder why we have fallen. We need to watch, to be alert! We are called to be soldiers—someone who is on guard the whole time. If we just pray and hope everything will turn out great, we are deceiving ourselves.

1. Why do you think Jesus told the disciples not only to pray but to "watch" in Matthew 26:41?
2. Which do you find hardest to watch; your eyes, ears, or heart?
3. Do you think it's possible to lose heaven because we are not alert and on our guard?
4. Why are our thoughts and passions so dangerous to us?

18

PASSIONATE AND PERSISTENT PRAYER

The prayer of a righteous person has great power as it is working.
–James 5:16

Cold prayers never speed. Prayer without passion is like a sacrifice without a fire. Prayer is a *"pouring out* [the] *soul"* to show passion (1 Sam. 1:15). Formality starves prayer.

"Fervent in spirit, serving the Lord." This is a metaphor taken from water when it bubbles and boils over. In the same way, our devotion should boil over in enthusiasm and passion (Rom. 12:11). The angels serve God with such passion and intensity that they are called seraphim—a Hebrew word that means to burn—to show they are all on fire, they burn in love and passion doing God's will (Psalm 104:4). Grace turns a Christian into a seraphim. Formality starves duty. Are the angels dull and cold when they serve

God? Duty without enthusiasm is like a sacrifice without fire. We should lift ourselves up to heaven in a fiery chariot of devotion.

Let us be enthusiastic and passionate in our duty of prayer. A dead form has no power. *"Because you are lukewarm, and neither hot nor cold, I will spit you out of my mouth"* (Rev. 3:16). Passion puts life into duty. "Fervent in spirit, serving God"—"boiling over." Jesus prayed *"more earnestly"* (Luke 22:44). When the fire on the golden incense burner was about to go out, Aaron had to put more coals on (Lev. 16:12). Incense was a type of prayer, burning coals of passion to show that the fire of passion must be put to the incense of prayer. Just so, praying with devotion is putting more coals to the incense.

It is not a formality—but passion and enthusiasm that will bring us to heaven. A formal prayer is like Ephraim, a cake not turned—hot on one side, but uncooked dough on the other. In the external part of God's worship, we might seem to be hot, but as for the spiritual part of God's worship, we are cold. If you want the kingdom of heaven, keep your heart and passion in what you do for the Lord. Elijah was carried up to heaven in a fiery chariot. In the same way, if you want to go to heaven, you must be carried there in the fiery chariot of passion. It is a persistent passion that takes hold of the kingdom of heaven.

You can never do too much for the kingdom of heaven. You cannot pray too much or love God too much. In secular things you can work too hard—you might kill yourself with work, but there is no fear of working too hard for heaven. "In righteousness, there is no need to fear excess," says Seneca.

The world is quick to subdue the godly as if they were too passionate and radical in their faith and belief. A person can follow the world too much, and be in too much of a hurry to be rich. A ferryman can take too many passengers into his boat, and it will sink. In the same way, a person can accumulate so much gold and silver that they sink themselves in unbelief (1 Tim. 6:9).

We can never be too sincere and passionate for the kingdom of heaven. There is no fear of being or doing too much in this regard. When we do all we can, we still fall short of the golden rule set for us, and of Jesus' golden example. When our faith is at its highest like the sun, there is still something lacking in our faith—all our work for the kingdom is never enough (1 Thess. 3:1). When Christians have done their best, they still have sins and needs to cry about.

Daily Reflection

Formal prayers have no heart in them. They have no passion and are dead with no life. These are not the kind of prayers God expects from us. He wants our hearts to be connected and alive when talking to Him. If we are sad, we can pray in tears. If we are angry, we can vent our frustration. He understands and wants reality, not carrying out rituals. Even more than that, He doesn't just want a once-off visit, but for us to be persistent and push in.

1. What is the difference between being passionate and emotional?

2. Why are prayers like burning incense, and can our prayers be more like that?
3. Why does the world mock and single out Christians who become too radical and passionate in their beliefs and duties?
4. Why can we never do or pray enough?
5. What kind of prayers do you pray? Are they rigid and cold or passionate and persistent?

19

PERSEVERE IN PRAYER

For you have need of endurance, so that when you have done the will of God you may receive what is promised.
–Hebrews 10:36

Jesus gives us more perseverance and helps us continue on to heaven through His intercession. He is an advocate as well as a guarantee. He prays that Christians will arrive safely at the kingdom. *"He is able to save to the uttermost those who draw near to God through him, since he always lives to make intercession for them"* (Heb. 7:25). The prayer He said for Peter on earth, He now prays in heaven for us; that our faith will not fail, and that we will be with Him where He is (Luke 22:32; John 17:24). And if He prays that we will be with Him in His kingdom, we cannot die along the way. Jesus' prayer is effective. If Christians' prayers have so much power in them, as Jacob, who had power with God, and Elijah who unlocked heaven by prayer—what has Jesus' prayer got? How can the children of such prayers go wrong and lose their way? How can we fall short of the kingdom, when we have Him praying for them, who is not only a Priest but a Son? What He prays for, He has the power to give because He is God.

But you might say that if perseverance is the only way to gain the kingdom, you are afraid you'll never get there. You're afraid of falling along the way, and the weak legs of your grace will never carry you to the kingdom of heaven. If you stood in your own strength, you might fall away. The branch that withers and dies has no root to grow from. You grow on Jesus the root, who will be strengthening you, even though you are weak in grace. Do not be worried about falling short of heaven: Because,

God has made a promise to weak believers. What is a bruised reed, but a picture of weak faith? Yet there is a promise—*"A bruised reed he will not break"* (Matt. 12:20). God has promised to supply the weak Christians with as much grace as they need until reaching heaven. Added to the two coins the good Samaritan left to pay to take care of the poor wounded man, he promised to also cover any costs of anything else that was needed (Luke 10:35). So, Jesus does not only give a little grace to us but his promise for more—He will give as much grace as we need until we get to heaven. *"The LORD will give grace and glory"*—a fresh supply of grace until we are perfected in glory (Psalm 84:11 KJV).

God takes care of weak Christians who are afraid they will not last until they get to heaven. Doesn't a mother look after the weakest child the most? *"He will gather the lambs in his arms; he will carry them in his bosom"* (Isaiah 40:11). If you think that you are so weak that you will never hold out until you get to heaven, you will be carried in the arms of the Almighty. He gathers the lambs in His arms. Jesus, the Lion of Judah, marches before His people, and His power holds them up so that none of them faint or die in their march to heaven.

"Hold me up, that I may be safe" (Psalm 119:117). Let us not rely on our own strength. When Peter cried to Jesus when he was on the water, *"Lord, save me,"* then Jesus took him by the hand (Matt. 14:30). When he grew too confident of his own strength, Jesus let him fall. Pray to God for persevering grace. A child is safe when held in the father's arms. In the same way, we are safe in Jesus' arms. Let us pray that God will put His fear in our hearts, and that we do not turn away from Him. Let us pray the same prayer Cyprian prayed, "Lord, perfect that which you have begun in me, that I may not suffer shipwreck when I am almost at heaven."

Daily Reflection

As humans, we often give up too quickly when we face resistance. It's not easy to keep on pushing when everything is against us. In prayer, however, we are called to be persistent and persevere. It's something God respects and rewards. Without this, we will never see results and never experience powerful, effective prayers. This doesn't mean carrying on and on without stopping in meaningless, cold prayer, but finding strength in Jesus to carry on until the door is opened.

1. Can you persevere in prayer for a long time, or do you find that you lose your way and become weak?
2. How does Jesus give us more perseverance?
3. What is God's promise to weak Christians, and how does this encourage and help us?
4. How does God take care of us when we are weak? How does this help us to persevere?
5. What does Ephesians 6:18 say about praying and perseverance?

20

A PRAYER OF SUBMISSION

Your will be done.
–Matthew 6:10

The eagle is not like other birds. Other birds cry for food when they are hungry, but the eagle does not make a noise, even though it has no food, because of the nobleness and greatness of its spirit. It is above other birds and has a spirit suitable to its nature. In the same way, the spirit of a Christian is so great that when he is going through hard times, he does not cry and whine as others do, but is silent, and lies quietly at God's feet. There is so much strength of grace in a Christian soul! When grace is crowning, it is easy to say, "Lord, your will be done," but when grace is conflicting, and meets with trials, then to say, *"Your will be done,"* is a glorious thing, and deserves a crown of honor.

A Christian prays, *"Your will be done."* It is the will of God that if troubles come, whether sickness, loss of belongings, or unruly children, God has allowed and ordered it. So, why don't we submit? Why are we discontent with what we pray for? We often forget our prayers, and even contradict them, when we pray *"Your will be done."* If not submitting to God is so unworthy of a Christian, shouldn't we make more effort to bring our wills to God's, and say, "Lord, let me do nothing unworthy of a Christian?"

Look at the attitude of lying at God's feet and saying, *"Your will be done."* A heart melted into God's will shows many virtues. As the holy ointment was made up of several aromatic spices, myrrh, cinnamon, and cassia, so this sweet attitude of the soul—submission to God's will in affliction—has a mixture of several graces (Exod. 30:23). There are three specific virtues we find: faith, love, humility.

1. **Faith**. Faith believes God does everything in mercy—that hardships and trials are to deal with some sin or to exercise some grace. Faith believes that God corrects in love and faithfulness (Psalm 119:75). If we believe this, it causes submission of our will to God.
2. **Love**. Love does not think of evil (1 Cor. 13:5). It takes everything that God does, in the best sense. It has good thoughts about God, which causes submission. "Let the righteous God take me through hardship," love says, "it will be a kindness, an excellent oil, which will not break my head!"

3. **Humility**. The humble heart looks at its sins and sees how much he has provoked God. He does not say that his hardships are great, but his sins are great. He lies low at God's feet and says, *"I will bear the indignation of the Lord because I have sinned against him"* (Micah 7:9).

A submissive attitude of the heart is full of grace—it is made up of several graces. God is pleased to see so many virtues all working together. He says the same about this Christian as David said about Goliath's sword, *"There is none like that; give it to me"* (1 Sam. 21:9).

The person who submits to God's will and says, *"Your will be done,"* not only shows many virtues but the strength of grace. It takes a lot of physical strength to be able to endure hard weather and not be changed by it. In the same way, to endure hard trials, and not fall away or worry, shows more than normal strength of grace. If you can say that you have brought your will into submission to God's will—that God's will and yours agree, as the copy and the original—then you have outstripped many Christians who have more knowledge than you. To be content to be at God's disposal, to be anything that God will have us, shows a noble, heroic soul.

Daily Reflection

Submitting to God is never easy. We want to say that God can have His way in our lives, but we always seem to hold onto something or take the steering wheel back. Our pride resists God having full authority to do what He wants, and not what we want. This is where surrendering comes in, laying everything down so He can rule and reign. It does not happen automatically and is a daily fight against the pride in our lives. That is why we need God's help, for Him to give us the grace and strength to surrender and submit.

1. Do you find it easy to submit to God—in everything?
2. Read Matthew 16:24. What does denying yourself have to do with submission to God?
3. Luke 9:23 says the same thing, but adds in the word "daily." Why is this important?
4. Why are faith, love, and humility the products of a submitted life?
5. Why do we need to pray for God to help us to submit to Him?

21

CONTENT WITH ASKING FOR DAILY BREAD

Give us this day our daily bread.
–Matthew 6:11

There are two rights to having the bread we pray for.

1. A spiritual right. In Jesus, we have a right as creatures, created beings who can call it "our bread." As we are believers, we have the best right to earthly things. *"All are yours."* By what right? *"You are Christ's"* (1 Cor 3:22-23).
2. A civil title, which the law gives us. To deny people a civil right to their possessions and make everything for everyone opens the door to anarchy and confusion.

See the privilege of believers. They have both a spiritual and a civil right to what they possess. Those who can say, "our

Father," can say, "our bread." Wicked men have a legal right to what they possess, but not a covenant right. They have it by providence, not by promise—with God's permission, not with His love. In God's eyes, wicked people are like those who take what is not theirs. All they have, their money and land, is taken but not paid for. The privilege of believers is that they can say, "our bread." Jesus is theirs—everything is theirs. How sweet is every bit of bread dipped in Jesus' blood! How delicious is that food, which is a promise of more! The meal in the cupboard is a promise of our angels' food in heaven. It is the privilege of Christians to have a right to earth and heaven.

Learn to be content with what God gives. If we have the necessities of life, let us rest satisfied. We pray only for bread; *"Give us this day our daily bread."* We do not pray for extras and delicacies, nor quails or venison, but for bread that can support life. Though we do not have as much as others—money and belongings—yet if we have bread to keep us from falling, let us be content. *"But if we have food and clothing, with these we will be content"* (1 Tim. 6:8). Most people are wrong in this sense. Though they pray that God would give them bread enough for them, they are not content with the amount. They greedily want more, and along with the daughters of the leech, cry, *"Give and Give"* (Prov. 30:15). This is an evil naturally in us.

Many people pray what Agur first prayed in Proverbs, "Don't give me poverty," but few pray his last prayer, "Don't give me riches" (Proverbs 30:8). They are not content with *"daily bread,"* but have the cancer of covetousness; they are still craving for more. *"He enlarges his desire as hell, and he is like death, and cannot be satisfied"* (Hab 2:5 NKJV). There are four things that are never satisfied: the grave, the barren womb, the thirsty desert, and the blazing fire. And I may add a fifth thing—the heart of a covetous person.

These people are not content with daily bread, but thirst insatiably for more. They will break over the hedge of God's command, and will not stop at sinning to get rich. Therefore, covetousness is called a radical evil. *"A root of all kinds of evils"* (1 Tim. 6:10). The Greek word for covetousness describes an excessive desire to get. Covetousness is not only in getting riches unjustly, but in loving them excessively, which is a key that opens the door to all sin. It causes

1. **Theft.** Achan's greedy heart made him steal the wedge of gold—it separated his soul from God (Josh. 7:21).
2. **Treason.** What made Judas betray Jesus? It was thirty pieces of silver! (Matt. 26:15).
3. **Murder.** It was the excessive love of the vineyard that made Ahab plan Naboth's death (1 Kings 21:13).
4. **Lies.** People will be covetous and also promise-breakers (2 Tim. 3:2). Love of silver will make people make a false promise, and break the same promise.
5. **Disloyalty.** *"Demas, in love with this present world, has deserted me"* (2 Tim. 4:10). He not only abandoned Paul but also his doctrine. Demas afterward became a priest in an idol temple of Dorotheus.
6. **Idolatry.** *"Covetousness, which is idolatry"* (Col. 3:5). Though the covetous person will not worship idols

and images in the church, he will worship the image on the coin.

Covetous people forget the prayer, *"Give us this day our daily bread."* They are not content with what is enough to satisfy them but are insatiable in their desire. Let us be aware of this cancer of covetousness! *"Keep your life free from love of money, and be content with what you have"* (Heb. 13:5).

Daily Reflection

We often strive to be content but forget that we need to repent of the covetousness in our hearts first. Our natural instinct is to want things and to want more. We are never satisfied with enough. And yet, that is often how God works, by giving us just the right amount to get through to the next day, not more and not less. Sometimes He overwhelms us in His abundance, but for the most part, it is just enough. Our appetites need to learn to be content with this and not want more and more. This attitude is what will see our prayers become less selfish and more fixed on what God really wants to give us.

1. Do you see yourself as a covetous person or not? Why do you say so?
2. Which part of Agur's prayer do you most associate with, asking that you will not be given poverty or asking that you will not be given wealth?
3. Why is it so hard for us humans to be content?
4. Read Luke 12:15 and Proverbs 15:16. What do you understand of these verses?

5. What is the promise that Matthew 6:33 gives us if we are content?

22

PRAYING FOR MORE THAN BREAD

Watch and pray that you may not enter into temptation.
The spirit indeed is willing, but the flesh is weak.
                    –Matthew 26:41

In the Lord's Prayer, there is one request for the body, *"Give us this day our daily bread,"* but two requests for the heart, *"Forgive us our debts… And lead us not into temptation, but deliver us from evil."* We should be more careful for our hearts than for our bodies, more careful for grace than for daily bread; and desire more to have our souls saved than our bodies fed.

- The soul is not a physical substance. It is a heavenly spark, lit by the breath of God. It is the more refined and spiritual part of a person. It has an angelic nature, a resemblance to God. The body is the more

humble part; it is only the casing, but the soul is the jewel. It is capable of communion with God in glory.
- The soul is immortal. It never expires. It can act without the body. Even though the body dissolves into dust, the soul lives (Luke 12:4). The essence of the soul is eternal. It has a beginning but no end. If the soul is so noble and dignified, then more care should be taken about it than the body. That is why we make one request for the body, but two for the soul.

As soon as Jesus said, *"Give us this day our daily bread,"* He adds, *"and forgive us."* He joins the request of forgiveness of sin immediately to the one of daily bread to show us that even though we have daily bread, it is nothing without forgiveness. If our sins are not forgiven, we cannot enjoy our food. Just as a person who is condemned takes little comfort from the food you bring them in prison, so, if we have daily bread, it will do us no good unless sin is forgiven. Though we have manna, which was called angels' food; though the rock pours out rivers of oil, it is all nothing unless sin is taken away. Daily bread can satisfy the appetite, but forgiveness of sin satisfies the conscience.

Why is this important in prayer?

It exposes the foolishness of most people, who, if they have daily bread—the delicious things of this life—they look no further; they are not concerned with forgiveness of sin. If they have whatever feeds them, they don't look at what should crown them. You can have daily bread and still die. The rich man in the gospel had daily bread—he had delicacies, and he *"feasted sumptuously every day,"* but in hell, he lifted up his eyes (Luke 16:19-23).

Let us pray that God would not give us our portion in this life, but that he would give forgiveness. This is the sauce that would make our bread taste even better. Do not be content with that which is common to animals—to have your hunger satisfied; but, more than daily bread, get forgiveness of sin. A drop of Jesus' blood, or a grain of forgiving mercy, is far more valuable than all the delights in the world. Daily bread may make us live comfortably, but forgiveness of sins will make us die comfortably.

Daily Reflection

Watson touches again on praying more for spiritual gifts than for physical ones. He looks at the Lord's Prayer and shows us what Jesus was teaching us in these few sentences. The fact that there are more requests for spiritual gains should encourage us in our own prayers to pray along similar lines. Instead of concentrating all our efforts on asking for what we need to sustain our physical bodies, we should be focusing on begging God to give us what we need to sustain our spiritual lives and hearts. To die spiritually is far worse than a physical death!

1. Why do you think people are more concerned with bread than forgiveness?
2. Why is the soul more important than the body?
3. How often do you pray for your heart and soul in

comparison with praying for things for your physical body, like food, health, and shelter?

4. Why do we need a realization of our sin and the judgment that awaits us to make us see how important spiritual prayers are?

5. What do you think would happen if you stopped asking God for physical needs and just asked for spiritual ones? Look again at Matthew 6:33.

23

PRAYER OF REPENTANCE

If we confess our sins, he is faithful and just to forgive us our sins and to cleanse us from all unrighteousness.
−1 John 1:9

Sin is not forgiven until it is repented of. Therefore, they are put together: Repentance and remission (Luke 24:47). As Fulgentius said, "Grant repentance, Lord, and afterward pardon." In repentance, there are three main ingredients, all of which must be before forgiveness. They are contrition, confession, and conversion.

Contrition

Brokenness of heart. *"Like doves of the valleys, all of them moaning, each one over his iniquity"* (Ezek. 7:16). This contrition, or breaking of the heart, is sometimes expressed by beating the chest (Luke 18:13); sometimes by tearing out the hair (Ezra

9:3); and sometimes by wetting the couch with tears (Psalm 6:6).

But not all humiliation is contrition. Some have only pretended to have sorrow for sin, and so they have missed forgiveness. Ahab humbled himself—his clothes were torn, but not his heart.

What is the real remorse and sorrow that goes before forgiveness of sin?

It is a holy sorrow; it is grieving for sin, because it is sin, dishonors God, and ruins the soul. Even if there was no suffering involved, the true penitent would grieve for sin. *"My sin is ever before me"* (Psalm 51:3). This contrition goes before remission. *I repented… I struck myself on the thigh; I was ashamed, yes, even humiliated… Is Ephraim My dear son?... I will surely have mercy on him"* (Jer. 31:19-20). Ephraim was troubled about sinning, and God's affections were troubled for Ephraim. The woman in the gospel stood at Jesus' feet weeping, and a pardon followed. *"Therefore I tell you, her sins, which are many, are forgiven"* (Luke 7:47 NKJV). A document seal is put on the wax when it melts—God seals his forgiveness on melting hearts.

Confession

"Against you, you only, have I sinned" (Psalm 51:4). This is not the type of spoken confession that the Catholics introduced, and believe that without confession of sins to a priest, no one can receive forgiveness. The Bible does not say this. *"Confess your sins to one another"* (James 5:16), is used as the

basis for Catholic confession, which would mean the priest must also confess to the people as they confess to the priest. The real meaning of that verse is that in public scandals, or private wrongs, confession must be made to others; but mainly, confession is to be made to God, who is the one offended. *"Against you, you only, have I sinned."*

Confession leads to sorrow. It must not be forced, sincere without reserve, passionate without hypocrisy—the heart must be in it. This makes way for forgiveness. *I said, "I will confess my transgressions... and you forgave... my sin"* (Psalm 32:5). When the tax collector and thief confessed, they had forgiveness. The tax collector beat his chest with contrition, and said, "God, be merciful to me, a sinner!" (Luke 18:13). There was a confession. He went away justified because there was forgiveness. The thief said, "We indeed [suffer] justly" (Luke 23:41). There was a confession. Jesus forgave him before he died. This story made Augustine say, "Confession shuts the mouth of hell, and opens the gate of paradise!"

Conversion

Turning from sin. *"We have sinned."* There was a confession. *"They put away the foreign gods."* There was conversion (Judges 10:15-16). It must be a complete turning from sin. *"Cast away from you all the transgressions"* (Ezek. 18:31). You would be reluctant if God only forgives some of your sins. If you want Him to forgive everything, won't you give up everything? Someone who hides one rebel is a traitor to the crown. The person who lives in one known sin is a traitorous hypocrite.

There must not only be a turning from sin but a turning to God. It is *"repentance toward God"* (Acts 20:21). The heart points toward God as the needle to the north pole. The prodigal not only left his partying but got up and went to his father (Luke 15:18). This repentance is the proper way to forgiveness. *"Let the wicked forsake his way… let him return to the Lord… he will abundantly pardon"* (Isaiah 55:7). A king will not forgive a rebel while he continues in open hostility. So, repentance goes before the remission of sin. Those who never repented, have no hope that their sins are forgiven.

God seals his pardons on melting hearts. Repentance makes us value forgiveness even more. The person who cries of their broken bones will value the mercy of having them set again.

Daily Reflection

Repentance is not something we do when we are born again and then never again. We do not turn away from sin, tell God how sorry we are, and ask for forgiveness only once in our lives. Unfortunately, it is more of a daily requirement, sometimes even more than once a day! Every sin we recognize should be brought to God with a penitent heart. Not arrogantly, but with contrition, knowing we do not deserve His forgiveness. Watson lays out three crucial elements for proper repentance here that can become part of our prayers if we want to have hearts that are right and clear before Him.

1. Why is contrition so important in repentance, and why should it come before confession?

2. Read Psalm 51:17. Why is a repentant heart described as contrite and broken?
3. If we don't have to confess to a priest, then who are we supposed to confess to?
4. Why is it not enough to be contrite and to confess? Why is conversion the ultimate step in repentance?
5. What is the difference between turning away from sin and turning to God?

24

FORGIVE US OUR SINS

Forgive us our debts.
–Matthew 6:12

From the word, *"forgive,"* we learn that the debt of sin is only removed by being forgiven. The false doctrine that we can pay a penalty to satisfy God, or that through our own works and effort, we can make up for our wrongs is incorrect! Those people intend to pay the debt they owe to God by themselves, and do not look to have it all forgiven. Why did Jesus teach us to pray *"Forgive us our debts"* if our own works and strength can satisfy God for the wrong we have done against Him? This false doctrine robs God of his glory, Jesus of his worth, and the soul of salvation! This belief makes us our own saviors, which is absurd because the obedience of a mortal being cannot satisfy an infinite offense. Sin being forgiven clearly shows we cannot do anything to repay the debt!

From the word *"forgive **us**,"* we learn that we must pray for forgiveness for ourselves. Even though we should pray for the pardon of others, *"Pray for one another,"* yet we are to beg for forgiveness for ourselves first (James 5:16). Will someone else's pardon do us any good? We must all put our own names in the pardon. A son cannot be forgiven by his father's pardon—he must have forgiveness for himself. In this way, it's okay to be selfish—everyone must get a pardon for their own sins. "Forgive us."

From the word *"**our**,"* we learn how just God is by Him punishing us. The verse says *"our debts."* We are not punished for other people's sins, but for our own. Augustine said, "No one has anything of his own, except his sin." There is nothing we can really call ours, but our sin. Our daily bread comes from God, but our daily sins come from ourselves. Sin is our own actions, a web of our own spinning. So, God is righteous in punishing us! We sow the seed, and God makes us reap what we sow. He will *"give every man according to his ways"* (Jer. 17:10). When we are punished, we taste the fruit of our own works.

From the next word, **"debts,"** we can see the enormous amount of sin we are guilty of. We do not pray "forgive us our debt," as if there was only a single debt, but sins, in the plural. There are so many sins that David cries out, *"Who can discern his errors?"* (Psalm 19:12). Our sins are like the drops of the sea, like the atoms in the sun—they are more than we can count. There are too many debts we owe to God for us to try and satisfy His justice. We should be so humbled to think how full of black spots our souls are that it makes seeking for the forgiveness of our sins.

As Rahab had to hang the scarlet cord in the window, so that when Joshua saw it he would not kill her, we must show the Lord the scarlet cord of Jesus' blood, because that is the way to mercy (Josh. 2:18). If God asked, "Why should I forgive you?" You can answer, "Lord, forgive me because You have promised it." And if He asks, "For whose sake should I forgive? You don't deserve it." You can reply, "Lord, for Your own name's sake. You said you will blot out sin for Your own name's sake" (Isaiah 43:25). "Your mercy will shine, and all Your other attributes will be exalted if You forgive me!"

So plead with God in prayer, and decide not to stop until your forgiveness is sealed. God cannot deny persistence, and He delights in mercy.

Daily Reflection

Watson takes a common verse that we all know so well and breaks it up word-for-word for us to examine even closer. In doing so, he highlights the importance of this simple but powerful prayer. When we understand the importance of forgiveness in our lives and why Jesus died to provide this incredible gift to us, we will ask for it more seriously and more often. It is not some add-on that comes with being a Christian, like a bonus gift for joining a club. Salvation rests on forgiveness, and without that, we will never get to heaven!

1. How often do you ask God for forgiveness? Not just for something you have done wrong, but for the sin and evil that hide in your heart.

2. Why is God just and right to punish us for our sins?
3. Why does Jesus use the word "debts" instead of "sins" in the Lord's Prayer?
4. What arguments can we use in asking for forgiveness that we actually don't even deserve?
5. Is it easier to ask for forgiveness from others or for yourself?

25

IN THE FACE OF TEMPTATION

Lead us not into temptation.
–Matthew 6:13

Satan is subtle. That's why we need to pray to God for wisdom to discern the traps of Satan, and the strength to resist them. We cannot stand against temptation on our own. If we could, the prayer would be unnecessary. We must not think we are clever enough to outwit the devil or escape his attacks. If David and Peter, who were pillars in God's temple, fell in temptation, how long before weak reeds like us are blown down on our own! Take Jesus' advice, *"Watch and pray that you may not enter into temptation"* (Matt. 26:41).

Jesus supports those who are tempted by interceding for them. When the devil is tempting, Jesus is praying. The prayer Jesus said for Peter when he was tempted is for all Christians. "Father," He says, "it is my child who is tempted!

Father, take pity on him!" (Luke 22:32). When a person is bleeding from wounds the devil has given him, Jesus shows them to his Father, and pleads for mercy. How powerful His prayer must be! He is heaven's favorite (John 11:42). He is the High Priest and a Son. If God could forget that Jesus was a Priest, he cannot forget that He is a Son. Jesus prays for nothing but what is in line with His Father's will. If a king's son asks only for what his father has decided to give, his request will not be denied.

One encouragement for us is that temptations bring out something good. They motivate a spirit of prayer in Christians. We pray more and better. Temptation brings us to pray. Maybe we came to God cold in prayer—we prayed as though we were not praying. Temptation is a cure for becoming too comfortable. When Paul had a messenger of Satan to buffet him, he was more sincere in prayer. *"Three times I pleaded with the Lord about this"* (2 Cor. 12:8). The thorn in his flesh was a spur in his sides to motivate him in prayer. When a deer is shot with a dart, it runs faster to the water. In the same way, a person who is shot with the fiery darts of temptation runs faster to the throne of grace; and is sincere with God, either to remove the tempter or to support him when he is tempted.

Overcoming Temptation

If you don't want to be overcome by temptation, be in prayer. People who walk in areas with contagious diseases carry antidotes with them—prayer is the best antidote against temptation. When Paul encourages us to *"put on the whole armor of*

God," he adds, *"praying at all times"* (Eph. 6:11, 18). Without prayer, the other weapons will not do much good. Jesus prescribes this remedy: *"Watch and pray that you may not enter into temptation"* (Mark 14:38). A Christian finds strength from heaven through prayer. Let us cry to God for help against the tempter, as Samson cried to heaven for help: *"O LORD GOD, please remember me and please strengthen me only this once, O God, that I may be avenged on the Philistines for my two eyes"* (Judges 16:28). *"And the house fell upon the lords and upon all the people who were in it"* (v. 30).

Prayer whips and torments the devil. Paul commands us to *"pray without ceasing"* (1 Thess. 5:17). This was the same advice Luther gave to a lady when she faced temptation, to fall on her knees in prayer. Prayer softens the force of temptation. Prayer is the best strategy we can use against the devil. Temptation might bruise our heel, but by prayer, we stand on the snake's head. When Paul had a messenger of Satan to buffet him, what remedy did he use? He turned to prayer (2 Cor. 12:8). When Satan attacks furiously, let us pray passionately.

If we don't want to be overcome by temptation, let us ask for help from others. If a house is on fire, wouldn't you call for help? Satan tempts so he can rob you of your soul. Let some friends know what you are struggling with, and ask for their advice and prayers. Who knows? Satan might be cast out by the combined prayers of others. In case of temptation, the prayers of Christians are very helpful.

If we don't want to be overcome by temptation, let us use every encouragement we can. If Satan is like a roaring lion,

Jesus is the lion of Judah. If Satan tempts, Jesus prays. If Satan is a snake to bite, Jesus is a bronze snake to heal. If the struggle is hard, keep your eyes on the crown (James 1:12). While we are fighting, Jesus will support us. When we overcome, he will crown us. What makes a soldier endure a bloody fight but the hope of a golden reward? God will soon call us off the field where the bullets of temptation fly so fast, and he will set a crown of glory on our heads. It will all be changed then. Instead of fighting, singing! Instead of a helmet, a crown! Instead of a sword, a palm branch of victory! Instead of armor, white robes! Instead of Satan's skirmishes, the embrace of a Savior! These eternal rewards should keep us from giving in to temptation. Who would give up a crown just to give in to lust?

Daily Reflection

Temptation is a part of life, even Jesus faced temptation. The tempter is always laying out his traps and snares hoping to catch us in them. But our natural eyes are not as clear and our human mind as discernable as Jesus' was, so we need all the help we can get. It's why this line was included in the Lord's Prayer when taught to the disciples. It's why we have it as a format or pattern for our own prayers—so we know we need to ask for help against temptation. Without God's help, we would fall headlong into the devil's traps all day long.

1. Why is it that people think they are clever enough to discern and avoid temptation on their own, without prayer?

2. Why can God not ignore Jesus' prayers for us?
3. What is the one good thing that temptations bring? Why is this good?
4. Why is prayer such a powerful antidote against temptation?
5. Do you find yourself praying more for help during temptation or more for forgiveness afterward?

26

DELIVERANCE FROM EVIL

Deliver us from evil.
–Matthew 6:13

Sin is such a deadly evil—the evil of evils. This is what we must pray to be delivered from, and it's regarding sin that Jesus taught us to pray, when He said, *"Deliver us from evil."* Hypocrites pray more against physical, temporary evils than spiritual ones. Pharaoh prayed more to have the plague of hail and thunder removed than his hard heart to be removed (Exod. 9:28). The Israelites prayed, *"Take away the serpents from us"* more than to have their sin taken away (Num. 21:7). The hypocrite's prayer is fleshly and carnal—they pray more to be cured of sickness than unbelief, more that God would take away pain than take away sin.

But our prayer should be, *"Deliver us from evil."* Spiritual prayers are the best. Are you sick? Pray more that the sickness of your heart will be removed than from your body. *"Heal me, for I have sinned against you"* (Psalm 41:4). The plague of the heart is worse than cancer in the chest. Are your children ill? Pray more to have their unholiness removed than their illness. Spiritual prayers are more pleasing to God and are music in His ears. Jesus taught us to pray against sin, *"Deliver us from evil."*

We must keep praying to keep us from falling into sin. *"Keep back your servant also from presumptuous sins"* (Psalm 19:13). We have no natural power in us to keep ourselves from evil. If we did, why would we need to pray to God for power? If David and Peter, who were strong, needed to ask for the Spirit to hold them up, how much more would we be in danger of falling, who have nothing but the power of free will to hold us up?

So, let us ask God for strength to keep us from sinning! Let us pray the prayer of David:

- *"Hold me up, that I may be safe"* (Psalm 119:117)
- *"Uphold my steps in Your paths,* that *my footsteps may not slip"* (Psalm 17:5 NKJV)
- *"Keep back Your servant also from presumptuous* sins" (Psalm 19:13 NKJV)
- *"Lord, whatever I suffer, keep me from sin!"*

A child is safe in the father's arms. We are only safe from falling into sin when we are held in the arms of Jesus. *"I give them eternal life, and they shall never perish; neither shall anyone snatch them out of My hand"* (John 10:28). In every trouble that comes against us, let us look to God for help and support. *"Should not a people inquire of their God?"* (Isaiah 8:19).

Only God Can Deliver

There are many who knock at the wrong door. When they are in trouble, they pray to the saints to deliver them. When they are in danger of a shipwreck, they pray to St. Nicholas. When they are sick, they pray to St. Petronilla! When they are in the pain of childbirth, they pray to St. Margaret. But this is wrong to call to saints in prayer. The Bible says, *"How then will they call on him in whom they have not believed?"* (Rom. 10:14). We cannot pray to anyone except those we believe in. We should not believe in any saint, therefore we cannot pray to him. In the Catholic prayer book, there are prayers for deliverance directed to Mary: "Deliver me, O Lady. O blessed Lady, in your hands our salvation is laid up." Isaiah 63:16 says, *"For you are our Father, though Abraham does not know us, and Israel does not acknowledge us; you, O Lord, are our Father, our Redeemer from of old is your name."* The saints and Mary do not know us.

To pray to saints is idolatry and blasphemy. Jesus taught us that in all our troubles we must pray to God for a cure. *"Deliver us from evil."* Only He knows what our troubles are and can help us from trouble. Only He who put the burden on can take it off. David went to God: *"Bring me out of my distresses"* (Psalm 25:17). With one word, God can heal. *"He sent out his word and healed them"* (Psalm 107:20). He delivered the three Hebrews out of the fiery furnace, Joseph out of prison, and Daniel out of the lions' den; which proves He is

God because no one can deliver as He does. *"There is no other god who is able to rescue in this way"* (Dan. 3:29). So, in all our troubles and needs, let us look to God, and say, *"Deliver us from evil."*

Daily Reflection

Temptation often leads to sin. It's a natural formula we find ourselves following because we were all born into sin. But it doesn't mean we have to follow that path simply due to the fact that it's what comes to us instinctively. That is why we need prayer, to be delivered from sin, to be kept from committing sins that we find ourselves naturally drawn to. Jesus added this into the Lord's Prayer knowing our continuous fight against sin would be impossible on our own—we need His help every day, every hour. Praying to be delivered should become as common to us as the number of times we face sin. These are prayers God wants to, and will, answer because they are spiritual and beneficial to our souls.

1. What is the difference between temptation and sin? Read James 1:14-15.
2. Why is God more ready to answer prayers to keep us from sin than to give us our daily bread?
3. Why is praying to saints and other holy people not correct according to the Bible?
4. Why is God the only one who can deliver us from sin?
5. Is praying for deliverance from sin a part of your daily prayers to God, or do you only pray this when you are already in trouble?

27

PRAYING TO BE DELIVERED

*When the righteous cry for help, the LORD hears
and delivers them out of all their troubles.*
—Psalm 34:17

In the prayer, *"Deliver us from evil,"* we pray to be delivered from the evil of our **heart**, that it may not entice us to sin. The heart is the poisoned fountain, where all actual sins flow from. *"For from within, out of the heart of man, come evil thoughts, sexual immorality, theft, murder, adultery, coveting, wickedness, deceit, sensuality, envy, slander, pride, foolishness"* (Mark 7:21-22). The cause of all evil lies in our own chest—all sin begins in the heart. Lust is first conceived in the heart, and then it is brought into the world. Where does rash anger come from? The heart sets the tongue on fire. The heart is a factory where all sin is contrived and produced. Therefore, how necessary is this prayer to deliver us from the evil of our hearts? The heart is the greatest seducer, which is why James says, *"Each person is tempted when he is lured and enticed by his own desire"* (James 1:14). The devil could not hurt us if our own hearts did not agree or allow it. All that he can do is to lay the bait—but it is our fault to swallow it!

Let us pray to be delivered from the lusts and deceits of our own hearts. Luther was more afraid of his heart than the pope or cardinal. Augustine prayed, "Lord, deliver me from myself!" One person gave their friend good advice by saying, "Beware of yourself!" Beware of your closest traitor, the flesh. The heart of a person is the Trojan horse, out of which comes a whole army of lusts.

In praying, *"Deliver us from evil,"* we pray to be delivered from the evil of **Satan**. He is *"the evil one"* (Matt. 13:19). How is Satan the evil one?

He was the first inventor of evil. He plotted the first treason (John 8:44).

His inclination is only to evil (Eph. 6:12).

His constant practice is doing evil (1 Peter 5:8).

He plays a part in all the evils and mischief that happen in the world.

He stops us from good. *"Then he showed me Joshua the high priest standing before the angel of the LORD, and Satan standing at his right hand to accuse him"* (Zech. 3:1).

He provokes us to evil. He put it into Ananias' heart to lie. *"Why has Satan filled your heart to lie to the Holy Spirit"* (Acts 5:3). The devil fans the fire of lust and strife. When people are proud, the old snake has poisoned them and puffed them up. The word "Satan" in Hebrew means an opponent or adversary.

He is a restless enemy. Spirits don't need sleep—he is always active, never resting. He *"prowls around"* (1 Peter 5:8). He doesn't walk like a traveler but as a spy. He looks to see where he can place his traps and attack us. Satan is a subtle contriver; there is no place that can protect us from his attacks. While we are praying, hearing, and meditating, he is in our company.

Satan is a mighty adversary, he is powerful. He is called the *"strong man"* (Luke 11:21). He captures people when he wants. They are *"captured by him to do his will"* (2 Tim. 2:26). The devil's work is to aim for our hearts with suitable baits. He lures the ambitious person with honor. He lures the covetous person with wealth. He lures the lustful person with beauty. Even though Satan may tempt us to sin, we pray that God would not allow us to say "yes." Even though Satan may attack the castle of our hearts, Lord, help us not to give up the keys of the castle to our mortal enemy. *"Be sober-minded; be watchful. Your adversary the devil prowls around like a roaring lion, seeking someone to devour"* (1 Peter 5:8).

When we pray, *"Deliver us from evil,"* it's to be delivered from the evil of the **world**. It is called an evil world. The world God made is good, but through our corruption it becomes evil, and we need to be delivered from an evil world. *"Who gave himself for our sins to deliver us from the present evil age, according to the will of our God and Father"* (Gal. 1:4).

We pray that God will prevent physical evils—our protection between us and danger. *"Save me from all my pursuers and deliver me"* (Psalm 7:1). We can pray against the plans of the wicked, that they may not work. *"Keep me from the trap that they have laid for me"* (Psalm 141:9).

We pray that God will deliver us out of physical evils—to remove His judgments from us. *"Remove your stroke from me"* (Psalm 39:10). We pray to be delivered from physical evils as much as God sees it good for us. We can pray to be delivered from the evil of sin completely, but we pray to be delivered from physical evils conditionally—so far as God sees fit for us, and may stand with His glory.

Daily Reflection

Prayer is not just talking to God, it is a lifeline, a siren to call for help. As humans, we are not as strong as we would like to think we are, especially when it comes to spiritual things, which is why we need emergency access to God. Like a first responder, He is always ready and willing to meet us in our hour of need and help us. This world is so full of evil that we cannot manage on our own. There is sin and evil around every corner. Worse, it is in our nature to be sinful! Being able to call out to Him, knowing He will be there the moment we ask, is a very necessary aid as we face whatever comes at us every day.

1. Why are our hearts so evil, even though we have been born again?
2. Read James 1:14-15. Notice that in this sequence of sinful events, the devil is not mentioned. Why is that?

3. It seems obvious that we would need to pray to be delivered from the devil. Are you afraid of him, or are you secure knowing God is stronger than the enemy?
4. Why do we need to pray against the world?
5. What has been your experience when praying for deliverance from certain sins and evil?

28

HUMILITY IN PRAYER

Humble yourselves before the Lord, and he will exalt you.
–James 4:10

Walk as Jesus did, in humility. His life was a pattern of humility. He was the heir of heaven, the Godhead was in him, yet He took *"the form of a servant"* (Phil. 2:7). For a Savior to become a servant; for the Lord of glory to lay aside His robe and put on rags; as if a king should leave His throne, and serve at the table! But that is not all. Jesus washes His disciples' feet. *"Then he poured water into a basin and began to wash the disciples' feet and to wipe them with the towel"* (John 13:5). No wonder it is said that He came in the form of a servant—he stands with His basin of water and a towel!

To express the depth of His humility, He was made in the likeness of men. Jesus lowered himself by becoming flesh! It took more humility for Jesus to humble himself to the womb than to the cross. It was not so much for the flesh to suffer, but for God to be made flesh—this was the wonder of humility! We read that Jesus' flesh is called a curtain: *"Through the curtain, that is, through his flesh"* (Heb. 10:20). By putting this dark veil or curtain on himself, He hid the glory of God. This was Jesus emptying himself (Phil. 2:7). The metaphor may extend to a vessel full of wine that is poured out; Jesus, in whom all fullness dwells, by humility was poured out as if there had been nothing left in him. This is a pattern of humility!

If you are looking for an eternal inheritance, walk in Jesus' steps—be humble! Grace shines brightest through the mask of humility! Humility makes us more beautiful. The humble Christian looks like a citizen of heaven. Humility is the veil of a Christian: Christ's bride never looks more beautiful in His eyes, than when she has on this veil of humility. *"Clothe yourselves, all of you, with humility"* (1 Peter 5:5).

Humility sweetens our duties. Incense smells the sweetest when it is beaten down into small pieces. When the incense of our duties is ground down small with humility, then it sends out its most fragrant perfume. The violet is a sweet flower—it hangs down its head so low that it can hardly be seen, and only reveals itself by its scent. This is the picture of humility.

The humble Christian studies his own unworthiness. He keeps one eye on grace to keep his heart happy, and the other eye on sin to keep it humble. The sin which keeps me humble is better than the duty which makes me proud! As humility hides others' mistakes, so it hides its own graces.

Humility looks at another's virtues and its own weaknesses. The humble person is one who does not only deny his evil things but his good things.

The humble Christian is no murmurer, yet he is always complaining. The more knowledge he has, the more he complains of ignorance. The more faith he has, the more he complains of unbelief. In short, the humble Christian translates all the glory from himself to Jesus. When he prays, he says, *"The Spirit helps us in our weakness"* (Rom. 8:26). When he mourns for sin, he says, *"God has made my heart faint"* (Job 23:16). When his heart is in a good attitude, he says, *"But by the grace of God I am what I am"* (1 Cor. 15:10). When he overcomes sin, he says, *"Through him who strengthens me"* (Phil. 4:13).

You who look for things above, let me tell you—the way to ascend is to descend! The lower the tree roots—the higher it shoots up! Do you want to shoot up in glory and be tall trees in the kingdom of God? Be deeply rooted in humility. Humility is compared by some to a valley. We must walk to heaven through this valley of humility. Hypocrites grow in knowledge—but not in humility. *"Knowledge puffs up"* (1 Cor. 8:1). The person who is proud of their knowledge, the devil does not care how much he knows. God hates the sin of pride. Be humble.

Daily Reflection

It seems obvious that we should be humble, not just in prayer but in everything. We know it, and yet it seems so hard to do or the last thing we get around to. But humility is the core attitude of a Christian. There are only two attitudes, and the other is pride, which God rejects. So, we need to pray for humility, pray in humility, and learn to be more humble each day. This is the heart that God gives grace. When we come with a surrendered heart, willing to obey God and not our own rights and plans, He will listen much quicker.

1. Why do you think it is easier for people to be proud than it is to be humble?
2. How did Jesus show us an example of humility while He was on earth?
3. How does humility change the way we pray?
4. Read James 4:10. Why does God only lift us up when we are down low?
5. Why is knowledge not regarded as the way to find grace with God?

29

PRAYING FOR OTHERS

To that end, keep alert with all perseverance, making supplication for all the saints.
–Ephesians 6:18

Why, in the Lord's Prayer, do we pray in the plural, "Give us"? Why do we not say, "Give me"?

It is to show that we should have a communal spirit in prayer. We must not only pray for ourselves but others. The law of God and the law of love bind us to this, we must love our neighbor as ourselves; therefore, we must pray for them as well as ourselves. Every good Christian has a shared feeling of the needs and suffering of others, and we pray that God would extend his abundance to them. We especially pray for other Christians. *"Making supplication for all the saints"* (Eph. 6:18). They are children of the family.

We should have a communal spirit in prayer. It keeps us from being narrow-spirited people, moving only within our own sphere; looking only at ourselves, and not worrying about others' issues; leaving others out of our prayers. If we have daily bread, we might not care if others starve; if we are clothed, we might not care that others go naked. Jesus taught us to pray for others, to say, "Give us," but selfish people are shut up within themselves, like a snail in its shell, and never say a word in prayer for others. They have no sympathy or pity.

Let us pray for others as well as for ourselves. A godly person benefits others as much as themselves. Spiders work only for themselves, but bees for the benefit of others. The more excellent anything is, the more it works for everyone's benefit. Springs refresh others with their crystal streams; the sun lights up others with its golden rays. In the same way, the more a Christian is given grace, the more they besiege heaven with prayers for others. If we are members of the body of Christ, we must sympathize with others in their needs, and this sympathy will lead us to pray for them. David had a communal spirit in prayer. *"Do good, O LORD, to those who are good"* (Psalm 125:4). Even though he begins the Psalm with prayer for himself, he ends with a prayer for others.

It is comforting for Christians who are going through tough times to know that they have the prayers of God's people for them; people who pray not only for the increase of others' faith, but that God will give them *"daily bread."* And even if they are in a good place with plenty, if they have the prayers of Christians for them around the world, they will benefit and thrive.

When a person's hardships and tough times are because they suffer for Jesus, they have the prayers of God's people. It is a huge privilege to have prayers in your favor; suffering Christians have a large share in the prayers of others. *"Peter was kept in prison, but earnest prayer for him was made to God by the church"* (Acts 12:5). What more could you ask for than to have God's promises and the prayers of other Christians? But when a person sins on purpose and does it scandalously, they have Christians' bitter tears and rebukes; that person is a burden to everyone that knows them, just as David says in another case: *"Those who see me in the street flee from me"* (Psalm 31:11).

Daily Reflection

We can easily pray for ourselves. It comes naturally to us to think of ourselves first and to ask for things that will help us. But, we are part of a family of God, part of the body of Christ. We cannot function on our own, looking after ourselves. It is why we are instructed to pray for others. Seeing others before ourselves is a key to humility and the way a Christian should operate. Putting other people's needs before our own should become a priority in our prayers.

1. Do you find it easier to pray for yourself or for other people?
2. Why is it comforting to know that others are praying for you?

3. How does this communal spirit of prayer help build us into a stronger, closer body of Christ?
4. What are the benefits for a church where the Christians are praying for each other?
5. What kind of prayers should we pray for our fellow brothers and sisters in Christ? Read Colossians 1:9 to see an example.

30

PRAYING FOR PASTORS

Brothers, pray for us.
–1 Thessalonians 5:25

Encourage God's ministers by being fruitful. When ministers are on the "mountaintop," let them not be on the rocks. I don't believe there was ever a time since the apostles that had a more educated, orthodox, powerful ministry than now. God's ministers are called stars (Rev. 1:20). Every morning a star shines in the Lord's bright constellation. How blessed we are as Christians to feed in the green pastures and to be fat and fertile; to be planted in the courts of God, and to flourish there (Psalm 92:13).

The best way to encourage your pastors is to let them see their efforts in your growth. It is good when a minister not only invites hearts but wins hearts. *"Whoever captures souls is wise"* (Prov. 11:30). This is a pastor's glory. *"For what is our hope or joy or crown of boasting before our Lord Jesus at his coming? Is it not you?"* (1 Thess. 2:19). A successful preacher wears two crowns; a crown of righteousness in heaven, and a crown of rejoicing here on earth.

Encourage your ministers by praying for them. Their work is great. It is a work that will take all of their heads and hearts. It is a work more suited for angels than men. *"Who is sufficient for these things?"* (2 Cor. 2:16). Pray for them! When Jesus went up the mountain and was going to preach, He did not need any of the people's prayers for him. He had the divine nature to supply Him, but all those who are in the ministry under Him, need prayer. If Paul, who was full of the grace of the Spirit and supernatural revelations, begged for prayer (1 Thess. 5:25), then surely other ministers who do not have any of those revelations need prayer.

And pray for your ministers that God will direct them what to preach, that he will cut out their work for them. *"Arise... call out against it the message that I tell you"* (Jonah 3:2). It is important to preach suitable truths, these are *"acceptable words"* (Eccl.12:10 NKJV).

Pray that God will go with them in their efforts, or else they work but catch nothing (Luke 5:5). God's Spirit must fill the sails of their ministry. It is not the hand that scatters the seed which makes it spring up, but the dew and influence of heaven. So it is not preaching, but the influence of the Spirit that makes grace grow in people's hearts. Pastors are just pipes and organs. It is God's Spirit blowing in them that makes the preaching of the Word capture hearts for Jesus. Ministers are only stars to light your way to Jesus. The Spirit is the magnet to attract you. All the good done by a pastor's ministry is "due to the Lord's excellent and effective working" (Bucer). So, pray for them, that God will make their work prosper in their hands. This may be one reason why the Word is not more effective when it is preached, because people do not pray more. Maybe you complain that the tool is dull, or the pastor is dead and cold. You should have sharpened him by your prayer. If you want to have the door of blessing opened to you through ministry, you must unlock it with the key of prayer.

Daily Reflection

If you are a pastor, you will know the encouragement of knowing your congregation is praying for you. If you are a member of a church, there is no greater support you can show your pastor than to be praying for him. Prayers go beyond physical help because it means that person is on your heart, and you are bringing them to God so He can bless and help them. Pastors and ministers need prayer more than most, since they are constantly on the frontline of a spiritual battle. They are just people like everyone else, facing temptations and dealing with pride, and they need prayer to stand strong and lead the people of God.

1. Have you ever thought that pastors need prayer so they can be directed on what to preach? Why is this important?
2. Do pastors need prayer, since they should be praying more than the rest of the congregation?

3. Read 2 Thessalonians 3:1. Look at Paul's request for the people to pray for him and the others preaching the gospel. What do you make of what he asks them to pray for?
4. Look at some of Paul's requests for prayer: Romans 15:30-32, 2 Corinthians 1:10-11, Ephesians 6:18-20, Philippians 1:19, Colossians 4:2-4, Philemon 1:22.

31

PRAY FOR UNITY

Behold, how good and pleasant it is when brothers dwell in unity!...
For there the LORD has commanded the blessing, life forevermore.
–Psalm 133:1, 3

God the Son is called the Prince of Peace (Isa. 9:6). He came into the world with a song of peace: *"And on earth peace"* (Luke 2:14). He left the world with a legacy of peace, *"Peace I leave with you; my peace I give to you"* (John 14:27). Jesus' sincere prayer was for peace; He prayed that His people might be one. Jesus not only prayed for peace, but bled for peace: *"Making peace by the blood of his cross"* (Col. 1:20). He did not only die to make peace between God and people but between people and people. Jesus suffered on the cross to cement Christians together with His blood. He prayed for peace, He paid for peace.

As there is one God, let us who serve Him be one. That is what Jesus prayed for. *"That they may all be one"* (John 17:21). How sad it is to see religion wearing a coat of different colors; to see Christians of so many opinions, and going so many different ways! It is Satan that has sown these weeds of division. He first divided people from God, and then one person from another.

In early church times, there was so much love among the believers that it made the unbelievers curious. Now, there is so little that it makes the Christians embarrassed.

Christians are Jesus' lambs. For a dog to worry a lamb is normal, but for one lamb to worry another is unnatural. A lack of love among Christians silences the Spirit of prayer. Hot emotions between people end in cold prayers. Where animosities and contentions continue, instead of praying one for another, Christians will be ready to pray against each other.

God puts His people together in hardship to bring them together in love. Metals will unite in a furnace. If Christians are to be united, it will be in the furnace of hardship. God's rebuke is a loud, *"Love one another"* (John 15:12). How wonderful it is when Christians are suffering together, to end up striving together!

"Do not speak evil against one another" (James 4:11). Some people do not create, they annihilate. They can annihilate the good in someone else quicker than they can imitate it. But, we are told to put on *"the breastplate of faith and love"* (1 Thess. 5:8). This breastplate may be shot at but it cannot be shot

through. *"Many waters cannot quench love, neither can floods drown it"* (Song 8:7).

Love will be the perfume and music of heaven. As perfect love drives out fear, so it drives out envy and division. Those Christians who could not live quietly together on earth will share love in heaven. The fire of strife will stop, there won't be any insults or backstabbing, but everyone will be tied together with the heartstrings of love. Satan cannot get in there to cause divisions. There will be perfect harmony, not one jarring note in the Christian's music.

One coal will warm and inflame another. So, when the heart is dead and frozen, the unity of Christians will help to warm it. *"Those who feared the LORD spoke with one another"* (Mal. 3:16). "Christians should never meet," says Mr. Boston, "without speaking of their meeting together in heaven." One Christian may be very helpful in prayer to another and give him a lift toward heaven. Many people have been strengthened and comforted by hearing another Christian's confession of faith. We read that when Moses' hands were heavy, and he was ready to let them fall, Aaron and Hur held them up (Exod. 17:12). A Christian who is ready to faint under temptation, and lets down the hands of their faith, is strengthened by other Christians' prayers, and their hands are held up.

A benefit of gathering together is receiving godly advice from others. "If a man," says Chrysostom, "who has only one head to advise him, could make that head a hundred, he would be very wise; but a single Christian has the benefit of the unity of saints, that they are as so many heads to advise him what to do in such a case." People usually travel faster when they are together with others. In the same way, we travel faster to heaven in the communion of saints.

Daily Reflection

Without unity, the church fails. It is no more than a club or a gathering of people interested in a sport or hobby and not each other. But Jesus prayed for His disciples that they would be united, because this would set them apart in the world. Unity and love are what sets the church apart from other groups. It is the beacon that should shine the brightest for other people to see, and draw them closer to God. God hates division and disunity, and a church that is fighting is not His plan for reaching out to the world. That is why we should pray more to be united and knit together with Christians.

1. Have you ever experienced or known about a church split or division that has been caused by Christians? Why does this happen?
2. How does God bring unity among brothers and sisters in Christ? Why is it not possible for us to achieve this on our own?
3. Love is the key ingredient in true unity. How do we get more love for others?
4. Do you find it easy to get along with everyone in your own church? Do you pray for God to help you to overcome differences?
5. Read 1 Corinthians 1:10. What do you understand about Paul's command?

ABOUT THOMAS WATSON

Thomas Watson was born in 1620, but the exact date and place of his birth are unknown. There is also little known about his childhood before he entered Emmanuel College, Cambridge. Here, his intellect and intense study helped him to flourish as he delved into botany, medicine, the classics, and theology.

After living in the house of Lady Mary Vere, the widow of Sir Horace Vere, Baron of Tilbury, he was finally appointed to a position to lecture and then preach at St. Stephen's, Walbrook in London in 1646. A year later, he married Abigail Beadle with whom he would have seven children (four of which died young).

During the outbreak of the Civil War, Watson became very vocal in his Presbyterian views and joined others in protesting against Charles I being executed. In 1651, he was involved in trying to restore Charles II to the throne and as a result, was imprisoned. After a year in jail, he was released and continued as pastor at Walbrook. His popularity and charm won him the respect of his congregants, and his church was always filled.

In 1662, the Restoration swept through the land, and Charles II came back from exile to take the throne. Although Watson had fought for his return, he found himself on the wrong side of the law, as the king made the Church of England the national church through the Act of Uniformity. As a result of his Presbyterian views, Watson's 16 years as pastor at Walbrook came to an abrupt end when he was formally ejected.

However, this did not stop him, and he began to preach in private wherever he was welcomed. After the Great Fire of London, Watson found a large room where he invited anyone to come and worship. It wasn't until 1672, once the Declaration of Indulgence came into effect, which allowed nonconformists to publicly and legally preach again, that he was able to secure Crosby Hall, Bishopsgate as his meeting place for the church. Along with Stephen Charnock, he preached there for a few years.

Watson's health became worse and he was forced to retire. In 1686, he died suddenly while praying on his own in his room.

His incredible writings and sermons are still published and read today, showing the incredible talent and inspiration he had for his insights into the Bible. *The Art of Divine Contentment, A Body of Divinity,* and *The Doctrine of Repentance* are just a few of the works he is still famous for, 340 years after his death.

BIBLIOGRAPHY

Crossway. (2001). *English standard version Bible*. Crossway Bibles.

Holman Bible Publishers. (2016). *The Holy Bible: NKJV new King James version*. Holman Bible Publishers.

Watson, T. (1978). *The Lord's Prayer*. The Banner Of Truth Trust.

Watson, T. (2017). *A body of practical divinity*. Forgotten Books.

Watson, T. (2021). *The Thomas Watson collection*. Antiquarius.

Watson, T., & Roth, J. (2017). *The art of divine contentment: In modern English*. Christian Classics for the Modern Reader.

www.ingramcontent.com/pod-product-compliance
Lightning Source LLC
LaVergne TN
LVHW010226070526
838199LV00062B/4747